We See Things They'll Never See

LOVE, HOPE, AND NEURODIVERSITY

CHANTELLE JESSICA LEWIS

JASON ARDAY

PRINCETON UNIVERSITY PRESS

PRINCETON & OXFORD

Published by Princeton University Press
41 William Street, Princeton, New Jersey 08540
99 Banbury Road, Oxford OX2 6JX

press.princeton.edu

GPSR Authorized Representative: Easy Access System Europe - Mustamäe tee 50, 10621 Tallinn, Estonia, gpsr.requests@easproject.com

ISBN 9780691262727
ISBN (paperback) 9780691262710
ISBN (e-book) 9780691263946

Library of Congress Control Number: 2024053820

British Library Cataloging-in-Publication Data is available

Editorial: Rebecca Brennan and Rebecca Binnie
Production Editorial: Terri O'Prey
Cover Design: Heather Hansen
Production: Lauren Reese
Publicity: Maria Whelan and Kathryn Stevens
Copyeditor: Maggie Studholme

Cover image: Ben Scott / Unsplash. The subject of the photo is Kuei Alor, who is a South Sudanese migrant who was photographed for the (Australian) National Photographic Portrait Prize. Kuei was sent to Kenya aged eight and lived in a refugee camp for twelve years, before gaining passage to Australia. She's now an actress and model. Makeup by Charlotte Ravet.

This book has been composed in Arno

10 9 8 7 6 5 4 3 2 1

WE SEE THINGS
THEY'LL NEVER SEE

For Gifty and Wendy

CONTENTS

"Hello to You out there in Normal Land"

Chantelle Jessica Lewis and Jason Arday

Hello to you out there in Normal Land
You may not comprehend my tale or understand
As I crawl past your window give me lucky looks
You can be my body but you'll never read my books

(IAN DURY, 1981)

From the imagined vineyards of Bordeaux, presumably, there might be many reasons to be cheerful, particularly when moving the body to and fro. In 1981, Ian Dury, an English singer-songwriter and commander of the punk and new wave era of rock music, was incensed by what the United Nations (UN) designated the "International Year of Disabled Persons," which was accompanied by the fetching tagline, "a wheelchair in every home." The patronising undertone was described by Dury at the time as "crashingly insensitive." His response was to write the song, "Spasticus Autisticus." In reference to this, Dury's friend Ed Speight christened Mr Autisticus "as the freed slave of the disabled," in a parody of Stanley Kubrick's film *Spartacus*. This protest has become the stuff of legend, with the song representing a battle cry, chiming with Dury's attempts, throughout his career, to reclaim and disrupt the language associated with disability.

"Spasticus Autisticus" stands as a poignant and powerful proclamation in the cultural landscape of disability rights and awareness that pre-dates the emergence of more contemporary and all-encompassing definitions, including, for example, neurodiversity. Amidst a whirlwind of socio-political movements, the song not only embodies the raw energy of punk rock but also acts as a vehicle for challenging societal perceptions of disability. Through his personal narrative and lived experience, Dury encapsulates the intricacies of living with a disability, interweaving a cleverly curated tapestry of irony, self-deprecation, and awareness.

At its core, Dury's offering reflects his own experiences of living with polio, which shaped his perspective on both his own identity and society's attitudes toward those with disabilities, where the ableist forecast was devoid of aspiration, love, and hope for the disabled community. The song is emblematic of the struggle for agency in a context often defined by pity and marginalization. Dury's choice to embrace the word "spastic," once a clinical term used to describe a type of movement disorder or condition characterised by increased muscle tone, resulting in a restricted muscle movement but later co-opted as a pejorative, demonstrates a rejection of disabling language and a reclamation of identity and capability in a way similar to this treatise, in which we challenge readers to either build on their existing knowledge or reconsider their understanding of neurodiversity and disability more broadly, moving beyond the straitjacket of neurodivergent stereotypes, which is funnelled through the dated and flawed medical model of disability.

As a frame for this discussion around love and hope, Dury's lyrics reveal a profound yearning for connection, disruption, and understanding. In its uncompromising wit and irony, the song evokes the complexities and limitations associated with disability, exploring themes of difference, rejection, dissonance, and acceptance. Dury's unapologetically outspoken and honest expression invites audiences to embrace difference, just as we invite our siblings to understand the importance of neurodiversity and of forming authentic relationships that reject societal prejudice.

Moreover, hope permeates Dury's work, encouraging a dialogue that counteracts the despair forecast for the "disabled" or the "blockheads" (the name of his band). By asserting his identity and challenging the status quo, Dury embodies the spirit of disruption and perseverance. This book, like his song, is intended as a rallying cry for self-acceptance, inclusion, and empowerment, capturing the essence of what it means to thrive, despite adversity, through the vehicle of love and hope. Dury's defiance is not just personal; it resonates with a wider movement that seeks to reshape the narrative around disability and our intersectional rights, liberties and freedoms. It inspires those who identify with the experience of being "othered" to embrace their identities fully and unapologetically, fostering a sense of community, belonging and support.

Neurodiversity, as a framework, further enriches the conversation surrounding Dury's response to the UN's overtly patronising incentive and intervention. In contemporary discourse, the ideas articulated in "Spasticus Autisticus" align seamlessly with the principles of this offering and the neurodiversity movement more generally. The growing recognition of neurodivergent perspectives has prompted a broader conversation concerning different types of intelligence and intellect. This shift encourages the acceptance and celebration of diverse ways of thinking, feeling, and being; an ethos that Dury perhaps unintentionally achieved in his attempts to provide a robust and ironic retort.

To foster a landscape in which love, hope, and neurodiversity thrive, it is essential to continue the conversation sparked by Dury's song. Advocates must persist in challenging prejudices and in championing the rights of individuals with disabilities. Education plays a pivotal role in this effort—by integrating discussions on disability, neurodiversity, and acceptance into our daily narratives, we can reshape perceptions and cultivate cultures of empathy.

In conclusion, Ian Dury's "Spasticus Autisticus" functions as more than just a song; it is a movement, a declaration of identity, and a catalyst for change. Its legacy lies in its ability to be utilized as a multifunctional tool in reframing ableist thought and language with regards to neurodiversity and disability in a manner that invites collective reflection and action. As we continue to navigate the complexities of neurodiversity, disability, and identity, let us draw inspiration from Dury's audacious spirit, by embracing the rich and often complex tapestry that comprises the human condition, thus advocating for a world where all voices are heard and celebrated. Through love and hope, we can create a future that honours the diverse narratives that define our shared humanity.

It is our hope that, at the very least, this book provides you with reasons to be cheerful and failing that you have our collective permission to hit us with your rhythm stick, but please do follow Dury's instruction by doing it slowly and quick. Enjoy the book with a shot of hope and a chaser of love.

With love always, CJ & Jay x

Come as You Are

Come as you are, as you were
As I want you to be
As a friend, as a friend
As an old enemy
(NIRVANA, 1991)

In its earlier versions, we planned to call this book "Come as You Are," the title of one of our favorite Nirvana songs, but also a lyric we felt captured perfectly our rallying call to our neurodivergent siblings from all over the world. The title "Come as You Are," meant a departure from adapting to the cultures and practices of the neurotypical majority and choosing to live lives true to ourselves. It captured our aspiration for everyone in society simply by saying that you are granted permission to live, just as you are. As the pioneering integrative medicinal and spiritual professor Deepak Chopra states in one of his Souls of Healing Affirmation meditations—"Today I will accept myself, just as I am. I will love myself—just as I am."[1] Acceptance by way of "coming as you are" is something the neurodiverse and disabled community is so often denied. We wanted this book to reflect this tension simply by showing that many of the consequences of neurotypical domination relate to its ongoing impact on personhood and social disconnection through everyday and more structured and institutionalized forms of ableism. We were drawing on examples of scholars such as Ramona M. Schwartz-Johnston, who showed that the systemic exclusion, from all parts of society, of people who *don't speak,* highlights just how culturally embedded exclusionary ideas of personhood and communication have become.[2] In this way, we wanted this book to reflect on the way embedded ideas about how people and society *should be* stops many of us being able *to be ourselves.*

As we began to develop the analysis, it was clear to us that our ambitions and arguments were more substantial than we had initially thought. Delving more deeply into existing work and activism surrounding both neurodiversity and disability justice, we found that the beauty of our experiences of navigating such an ableist world could be found in the mechanisms we had collectively acquired to create better lives for ourselves— lives that transcend simply surviving. As Ema Loja, Maria Emília Costa, Bill Hughes, and Isabel Menezes have contended, the path towards deconstructing the demeaning imaginary and practices of ableism must be led by disabled people through an embodied politics.[3] By embodied, we mean the lived, felt, and physical experience of what it means to navigate ableism and disability. These authors triggered the foundations of our arguments in that we became inspired by looking at how we ourselves live through and resist ableism in our everyday lives. It was crucial to look carefully at our own repetitions and routines, and at how we respond and react in our professional and personal lives. Like many others in the global neurodiversity movement, we made space for ourselves by being incredibly adaptable and understanding of others; by planning and organizing around our neurodivergence; by finding ways to keep up with our neurotypical or able-bodied siblings. We have a deep understanding of the uncertainties of life and all its disappointments, victories, and ordinariness. We have characteristics formed through our lived experiences that can provide *lessons for living for everyone.* We started to see how understanding neurodiversity produces a politics that goes beyond "coming as you are." Neurodivergence produces a way of seeing the world and of understanding our social lives that can benefit everyone. To come as you are is to be given the freedom to live an ordinary and dignified life. But to get to the point of coming as you are requires work to expose and dismantle the structures that impact everyone's ability to be themselves. With these formative reflections about what this book is trying to say, we knew we needed a new song lyric. Inspired by the old adage that necessity is the mother of invention, the words of wisdom whispered to Jason during his lengthy evening showers came from Burnage's finest, the architects of "Madchester"—Oasis. With their legendary and generation-defining offerings from the anthemic "Live Forever," we have been able to show that the true objective of this book is to demonstrate that as neurodivergent and disabled people, "we see things they'll never see," and our experiences can help to shape a more equitable society for *everyone.*[45]

ACKNOWLEDGEMENTS

Chantelle

I would like to begin this section by acknowledging my incredible co-author, bestie and brother, Professor Jason Arday! One of the greatest gifts a person can give you is the space to *be yourself.* Jay, you give me just that, over and over again. Our relationship and our process of creating together has helped to unlock a part of me that I would so often hide. Through our love of music, popular culture, THE NEWS and THE DISCOURSE, you taught me about the beauty of the heterogeneous nature of the Black experience. You encouraged me to give myself permission to just be; to allow myself to sit in my quirky and mad self. For me, stepping into authenticity has required several cheerleaders along the way; and Jay, you have led this and persuaded me to see myself in ways I never knew possible.

Writing this book with you has been such a beautiful experience. This was an exceptionally therapeutic process and helped me to "get back on the horse" when it came to my writing and creativity. You came into my life and brought so much love, laughter, happiness and support. You have been one of my angels, Jay! Meeting people that you can collaborate with in such a meaningful way is an immense privilege. The love we share is something I will always cherish. You came into my life for reasons this acknowledgement section can't really capture and the love we share for each other, as we always say, is *more than words.*

I hope our readers enjoy what we created together because we definitely had a lot of fun making it!

To Jen Gates and Becca Brennan—thank you for believing in our vision for this book.

I am really grateful to my stepdaughters, Evelyn and Becky Miller. You guys keep me on my toes, have kept me grounded and have been such a guiding light throughout my adult life thus far. Huge thank you to special friends and family in my life for believing in me and supporting me—Beth and Jack Daley, Paulette Williams, Ez Chigbo, Anna-Marie DeSouza, Hannah Lawal, Lavinia Webster, George Ofori—Addo, Tiphaine Liechti-Moxon, Katie Smith, Gemma Cottis, Hayley Dallow, Kathryn Medien, Ricia Leslie, Denise Marshall, and all the people in Islington Healing Network, Citygate Church (Beckenham), Aaron Lowe, Lauren Rostrup, Hans Rostrup, Kyle Swaby, Dunni Dickie-Johnson, Lemuel Dickie-Johnson, Yemi Alade, Tola Alade, Gabriel Sekyere-Afriyie, and Akin Lawal.

Thank you to colleagues and friends for the academic guidance—Maggie Studholme, Bev Skeggs, Levi Gahman, Michaela Benson, Les Back, Emma Jackson, Karen O'Reilly, Stephen Tuck, Alana Lentin, Caine Lewin-Turner, Aaron Winter, Holly Cooper, Francesca Sobande, Patricia Daley, Julia Toppin, and Rita Gayle.

Big thank you to my dad and mum, George Lewis and Wendy Nye, for bringing me into this world and instilling in me a sense of purpose, love and social justice from a very young age! Thank you to my grandparents, Brenda Foord and Alan Foord, for all the love, care and support. Special thank you to my favorite aunties, Sharon Stapleton and Patricia Brown, and my uncle Andrew Stapleton. Thank you also to my little sister Germaine Thompson for blessing this world with your beautiful spirit.

Finally, thank you to my late husband, Matt Miller, for being the catalyst for opening my heart in ways I never knew possible.

Jason

I would like to extend my sincerest thanks to Jennifer Gates and Rebecca Brennan for their guiding hand and unwavering belief throughout. The biggest thanks goes to the truly exceptional Dr Chantelle Jessica Lewis. It has always been the greatest privilege to work by your side. You embody the very best of what society can truly offer when love, heart and mind are set to inspired purpose. I dedicate this book to your enduring and inspiring brilliance. I love you more than words can express.

It is my sincerest wish and hope that all readers, siblings, and allies continue to take heart whilst setting their hands to greater purpose in creating a more loving and inclusive society.

PLAYLIST

Pulp—Something Changed
Dire Straits—Sultans of Swing
Bob Marley—Concrete Jungle
Ocean Colour Scene—The Day We Caught the Train
Michael Jackson—Blood on the Dancefloor
Space—Avenging Angels
Martha and the Muffins—Echo Beach
Fleetwood Mac—Silver Springs
Santana—Let the Children Play
Simon and Garfunkel—Scarborough Fair
Blur—This as a Low
The Stone Roses—Made of Stone

1

Sowing the Seeds of Love

Time to eat all your words
Swallow your pride
Open your eyes

(TEARS FOR FEARS, 1989)

Introduction

Characterized by its use of synthesizers, electronic instruments, penetrative rhythms, and catchy melodies, synth-pop defined a generation of musicians and creatives in the 1980s. The architects of the genre were bands like Soft Cell, Kraftwerk and The Human League. It was propelled into the mainstream, however, by the bands that would come to depict the sound of the decade: Depeche Mode, New Order, and of course Smith and Orzabal, better known as Tears for Fears.

The Bath duo, whose original incarnation was the mod-inspired Graduate, orchestrated a sound that was synonymous with continuous evolution. Maturing from songs such as "Change," which Orzabal famously describes as "not really being about much" to the politically conscious "Sowing the

Seeds of Love," itself heralded by reviewers at the time as a pastiche of The Beatles, Orzabal's fleeting interest in politics towards the end of the 1980s would become the Somerset pair's most overtly political offering. Driven by the egalitarian vehicle of socialism, the message of this song—infused with incensed calls for the removal of the destructive British Conservative Government of the time—mirrors many of the global and domestic problems we are currently facing.

The many muses from whom we have drawn our inspiration are a particularly important aspect of this treatise, and just as in other areas of life imitation remains the sincerest form of flattery. In the same way, the christening of this track ("Sowing the Seeds of Love") was inspired by Cecil Sharp and was ultimately a nod to his own melodic offering, "The Seeds of Love." Reflecting this well-trodden path of imitation (flattery) encourages a thread of inspiration that pays homage to Smith and Orzabal's ideal. We use their words as both a navigational and a moral compass in an attempt to signpost our societal siblings towards a collective sowing of loving seeds throughout this opening chapter. We do so in the hope that it becomes a conduit for conveying a broader message, which situates love as the catalyst for change whilst encouraging the continual watering of these seeds until they bloom. We also recognize the might of the nib in being able, like Tears for Fears, to form words (lyrics) that reject the constrictions of an unjust, neurotypical society and which also—perhaps equally importantly—constitute a call to arms, a call to make a stand while shaking up the views of ordinary people.

Now, let's get into it. We have drawn on our lived experiences of neurodivergence, Blackness and class (see below), as well as our sociological training and imagination, to produce a contribution to activism, advocacy, and writing that aims to provide routes into exposing and dismantling neurotypical power and domination. We home in on the way everyday life is so often structured around rigid ideas of what "normal" looks and sounds like and locate these cultures in historical and contemporary depictions of other social inequities (for example racism and classism). In an effort to show how the neurodiversity movement (see below) can offer solutions for some of society's biggest injustices, we trust the reader to look at how theories of love and knowledge are vital ingredients for creating and imagining a truly inclusive society.

In this book you will find a critical yet hopeful and loving dialogue about how the neurodiversity movement is enhanced for everyone when we take notice of the way power becomes organized through race, class, and gender primarily. It is a call to action for the powers that be, as well as a book about understanding, acceptance, and humility. It is a book that has been put together in an effort to take stock of how history continues to inform the ways we understand each other and the reflexive strategies required to make space for different ways of being and understanding the world. The key issues we cover here relate to the locally and globally felt uneven distribution of resources, and the way power evolves to protect and maintain ideas around who should be considered the "normal" or "ideal" citizen. Our intention is to show how the politics of neurodiversity and the neurodiversity paradigm more broadly can help us understand global inequities in a way that can offer multiclassed and multiethnic solidarities across difference.

We have intentionally written this book in a way that uses theories that some people might not have come across before. We see it as an example of the sort of conversation that needs to extend beyond the university (and academia in general) and thus encourage a culture where processes like "methodology" (how we come to understand and research) are universal concepts we can all learn and include in our dialogues about society. While we make a conscious effort, throughout the book, to both explain and explore the academic language that might put some readers off, we do need to make clear that one of the key uses of terminology we home in on was inspired by the work of autistic sociologist and neurodiversity advocate Elizabeth Radulski from La Trobe University, in a 2022 paper titled *Conceptualising Autistic Masking, Camouflaging, and Neurotypical Privilege: Towards a Minority Group Model of Neurodiversity*. Radulski's work was the first place we really started to see a discussion of some of our own personal reflections about race, ableism, and capitalism (spoiler alert!). In particular, Radulski's clear and concise conceptualization of "neurotypical hegemony" (see later in this chapter) as the social processes by which *"the neurological majority have the benefit of shaping cultural norms for society and communication that reflect their own traits and characteristics"* guided a lot of the themes we have used to piece together the arguments in this book.[1] We hope to pay homage to the many scholars and advocates who have paved the way for arguments that incorporate freedom for us all but—for us personally—Radulski's formative work certainly deserves an honorary mention here.

With voices and advocacy like that of Radulski's, our overarching ambition has been to show that existing sociological work and decades of advocacy intervention across a broad range of themes related to both disability and neurodiversity and their intersections, can be channelled to better imagine a more equitable future for all groups of people. In writing this book, we see how intentionally paying attention to the politics of neurodiversity and disability justice more broadly offers the chance to build a new culture with a collective spirit of love, hope, and solidarity. Written in language that shows sensitivity and strength, the objective of this book is that all readers should come away with an analysis of society and its people that is grounded in a *critical yet loving framework of understanding*. We are guided by much of bell hooks' scholarship, which centers the inextricable link between love and liberation. All roads should lead us to a synchronization between the practice of love and the routes to freedom. We are moving towards ways of living and understanding each other which recognize that domination in all its forms should be understood through what hooks describes as "anti-love."[2] To resist the cultures of "anti-love" and to actualize and become *loving*, our contributions in this book provide us with the knowledge to garner a type of empathy that can be applied to all our relationships. Whether these relationships are with our families, communities, or colleagues, or with people we would consider strangers—this is about producing a relational politics attentive to the historical and contemporary structuring of society to generate equitable futures for everyone. This civic responsibility stems from our belief that to know where you are going, you need to know where you have come from. We adopt this philosophy as a navigational tool for the essential mapping of where we need to go as a society.

Our primary mechanism for engaging with such vast and expansive intentions is located in the emancipatory politics of neurodiversity, alongside a multifaceted engagement with the perils of neurotypical hegemony and domination (see later in this chapter). This book has been constructed with our lived experiences of being Black and neurodivergent people as a starting point. This means that the overlaps between ableism, racism, and capitalism in particular have been grounded in our subjectivities, as we move between different social worlds.

Thankfully, we stand on the shoulders of giants; collectives comprised of the writers, creatives, activists, parents, siblings, and young people at the vanguard of the push to abandon reductive and deficit language and treatment of all people. Zooming in on lived experiences of the struggle to be valued in society, we are grateful for dialectics of hope and hopelessness (when things go wrong) to keep us grounded in this work. If we are to truly understand ableism, capitalism, and racism as some of the central aspects of domination, we have to find moments of solace, since the scale of the task at hand is vast, and the road to liberation can be rough as well as smooth. As Gabor Maté notes in *Scattered Minds: The Origins and Healing of Attention Deficit Disorder*, compassionate patience has to include a tolerance for failure.[3] Such juxtapositions are integral to dialogues and practices for transformational disability justice. As scholars like Fiona A. Kumari Campbell suggest, "we are all, regardless of our subject positions, shaped and formed by the politics of ableism."[4] In a similar vein, she collectivizes this struggle by stating that,

> The experience of disablement can, arguably, be spoken of not in terms of individualized personal tragedy but in terms of communal trauma, where the legacies of ableism pervade both the conscious and unconscious realms.[5]

While we see Campbell here as stressing a trauma felt collectively by the global disability community, we also believe this trauma can be located in cultures reproduced across the whole of society. In the way described above, communal trauma is of course more intensely felt by others, but its very existence, and the varying ways and guises in which it manifests—through illness, poverty, racism, and sexism for example—show that these are challenges which should be understood as societal, and therefore as matters for us all to contend with. No one is free until everyone is free.

In this book we show how ableism is embedded in how we think about education, health, employment, and family life.

Our route into this work is located in an engagement with neurodiversity in all its intersectional modalities, providing radical opportunities to create new cultures of understanding that are liberating for everyone. Race, class, ethnicity, gender, and nation are just some of the social structures for which the politics of neurodiversity can produce an emancipatory analysis. Social justice, for us, is the view that everyone deserves equitable economic, political, and societal rights and opportunities. In *Black, Brilliant and Dyslexic*, Marcia Brissett-Bailey notes that the role of neurodiversity advocates now is about *breaking down the silences* of difference through representation, support, and evidence.[6] Brissett-Bailey argues that without a more thorough commitment to addressing the ethnicized, classed, and gendered dynamics of neurodiversity, we continue to create systemic barriers between families, in education, and in the workplace. With these types of wisdoms embedded in each page of this book for the twenty-first century, we and many others believe that the politics of neurodiversity is a matter for social justice in relation to the way we relate to, understand, and live with each other, that appreciates difference and humbly allows for the emergence of understanding and empathetic cultures.

In this introductory chapter we lay out the political motivations behind the book. We do this by emphasizing the importance of the collective when it comes to social and disability justice. We then talk about how we came to write this book by stretching the muscles of our existing professional relationship and friendship. Our discussions then lead us to contextualize social and material inequalities on a local and global scale. In the second half of the chapter we begin to introduce concepts such as neurotypical hegemony, Black subjectivities and Marxism. Woven throughout these introductory provocations are the importance of love and political education, as well as of going beyond the politics of representation.

Neurodiversity, Neurotypical Society, and Disability

Before we get into exactly how we are all getting free, we are going to start as we mean to go on by doing our absolute best to explain how we are using the concepts and terminology found throughout this book. As "neurodiversity" has become a bit of a buzzword, we see it as our responsibility to be very clear about how we are using the term in this book. We want to caveat this introduction by disclosing that we ourselves can still do better when it comes to the language and terminology of neurodiversity, neurotypical society, and disability. With this, we remain profoundly grateful to individuals and collectives in the neurodiversity movement, as well as to critical friends and colleagues who continue to "check our workings out." The politics of critical love and understanding embedded in the pages and production of this book are what motivates us to encourage people to step into unknowing, not knowing, or not quite being sure as means to lean into openness, humility, and learning. As long as we are willing to admit when we have missed the mark and have the appetite to do better, we are onto a winner!

Now, first and foremost—what exactly do we mean by neurodiversity? Our—understanding and use of the term neurodiversity has been inspired by the author, educator, queer futurist, and transpersonal somatic psychologist, Nicky Walker. In his book *Neuroqueer Heresies*, he carefully lays out three key areas of definition and terminology for those of us seeking to understand, contribute and advocate for both neurological inclusion and diversity.

Throughout the book, we invariably draw on Walker's definition of neurodiversity as:

i. "the diversity of human minds, [and] the infinite variation in neurocognitive functioning within our species."

Secondly, when we refer to neurodiversity, we are describing:

ii. a collective political and social project and movement which contains a variety of neurodivergent individuals and groups with different goals, viewpoints and affiliations (more on neurodivergence below).

Thirdly, the discussions found throughout the book are very much a contribution to the *neurodiversity paradigm*, which asserts that:

iii. There is no normal, right or healthy type of brain.

Finally, we are guided by Walker's assertion that:

iv. neurodiversity creates social dynamics (and inequalities) that are socially produced like other structures and identities of difference such as ethnicity, class, and gender.

Next, we note the indomitable contribution to terminology and language in the neurodiversity movement of radically neurodivergent activist, Kassiane Asasumasu. Asasumasu's coining of terminology came out of the autism rights movement of the 1990s, in which it was claimed that a wide range of people experienced the world in a way similar to autistic people yet were not actually autistic. In 2000, Asasumasu's blog, "Radical Neurodivergence Speaking," provided us with the terminology "neurodivergent" and "neurodivergence." In short, when a person or group diverges from what society has considered to be "normal" or "neurotypical" cognitive functioning, this individual or group is neurodivergent. Neurodivergence on the other hand is a way for an individual or group to describe how their trait or traits show up. For example, neurodivergence ranges from Autism or Autism Spectrum Conditions to ADHD (Attention Deficit Hyperactivity Disorder), ADD (Attention Deficit Disorder), dyslexia, dyspraxia or Developmental Coordination Disorder (DCD), dyscalculia, cognitive functioning difficulties or executive dysfunction, dysgraphia, misophonia, slow processing speed, global development delay, stammering, Tourette's syndrome, traumatic brain injury, and Post-Traumatic Stress Disorder (PTSD). In line with Asasumasu's assertion of a broader understanding of neurological difference, we also align ourselves with her inclusion of mental illness in neurodivergence (see chapter 3).

We are also in agreement with Robert Chapman that leaning into a categorization of neurodivergence (and neurodivergent traits) is part of reclaiming them from the oppressive and eugenicist practices of the discipline of psychiatry.[7] The neurodiversity movement continues to provide us with the language to show how a "minority mode" of neurocognitive functioning *becomes* disabled by a dominating neurotypical ("normal") society.[8] In such a society, we are different simply because society has decided what is *normal* (don't worry—more explanation of this to come). By contrast, neurotypical (or "normal") society is a cultural and social reproduction that is not fixed by people's individual profiles or characteristics. Neurotypical culture refers to sets of behavioral expectations socially developed in line with dominant ideas about neurological functioning that normalize certain organizational, social, and emotional practices as the correct and conventional way to be. Is neurodivergence a disability? For our presentation throughout this book, informed by our sociological training and lived experience, the short answer is yes. While we demonstrate the disabling features of neurotypical society, we want to acknowledge those at some of the sharper ends of the spectrum of disability and neurodivergence; the physically impaired or compromised, those unable to properly communicate their needs without external support, and of course our nonverbal siblings. We have chosen to contribute to the connectedness, fluidity, and unification of social justice movements with an interchangeable reference to disability and neurodiversity throughout, aligned with the social model of disability. While we recognize some of the conceptual and practical (and perhaps ethical) flaws of presenting neurodiversity and disability in tandem, we are overwhelmingly inspired by the possibility of a solidarity that spans our differences. Working with and through that which sets us apart is a way of building love and understanding in the face of consistent and multiple sites of struggle. In this way, our contribution is built in resistance and opposition to the medical model of disability and neurodiversity by playing close attention to the possibilities of a social model which takes seriously the impact of physical, attitudinal, communication, and social barriers which are not "natural," but are rather created and constructed around us.[9] This contribution is built in alliance with the neurodiversity movement, which opposes the idea that certain neurological conditions are inherently "abnormal" or "disordered." This is about building a framework that seeks to change society into something more inclusive and accommodating for all.

Many thanks for bearing with us through these the introductory notes on definitions, labels, and categories. We recognize their possibilities and limitations, yet we remain persuaded by the merits of working with terminologies that address difference, because whether they are used or not, they have the power to have lasting impacts on our life courses.

Visions for Social and Disability Justice

We are public sociologists, which means that our usual way of talking about social justice focuses on how *we can take people with us* to learn together about how to improve the lives of the majority.[10] Taking people with us requires the long and challenging process of moving beyond feelings and building our understandings of life and society around facts, truths, and histories. This is not about denying people their individual experiences or the emotions attached to them, but more about emphasizing that in order to build collective strength and solidarity we need space to make mistakes, grow, and connect through our shared histories and identities. This work is lifelong; it is difficult, overwhelming, beautiful, and all-consuming all at once. Grounding ourselves in openness, humility, and care in our efforts to find pockets of hope and solidarity fuels the politics of this book. We operate from the premise that "telling ain't selling," and that broadly speaking, people are doing their best with the information they have to hand. Returning again to bell hooks, we stress that arriving where we are, or recognizing a lack of loving and understanding of ourselves and others usually occurs because "[we] were socialized to see [ourselves] as unlovable by forces outside [our] control."[11] We can always do better to understand how society is organized and our job, as public sociologists, is to point out knowledge and research to help people to have a better understanding of the society we find ourselves in. This is clearly not the only method of political education, but it is the role we have both chosen. We are grounded in the tradition of our foreparents, among whom bell hooks, Claudia Jones, Olive Morris, Robin D. G. Kelley, Audre Lorde, Maya Angelou, Paulo Freire, Angela Davis, Sylvia Wynter, Katherine McKitterick, Antonio

Gramsci, C. Wright Mills, Gabor Maté, Raymond Williams, Alana Lentin, Gail Lewis, Frantz Fanon, Patricia Hill Collins, Cedric Robinson, Walter Rodney, and of course, Stuart Hall, have always stood out for us in terms of their commitment to understanding and communicating the importance of everyday life in how we articulate anti-capitalist, anticolonial, feminist, and now neurodivergent futures. Though each of them has their own variation on "how we get there," we have been inspired by their philosophies around the importance of educating the masses and really taking the time to help people imagine a better world. Of course, most of these theorists are marked by their Marxist, Black feminist, and mostly humanist endeavors, which we hope to have woven through our presentation of love, hope, neurodiversity, and the possibilities of knowledge production in this book.

The book is for anyone who wants to join us in creating a world where everyone is given the space to both understand and be themselves. The stories, research, and conversations on which we draw have been put together to show how creating a collective culture of love and hope can build a society truly inclusive of disability and neurodiversity. We aspire to a world that centers the needs of neurominorities as a way to make our ways of being and existing ordinary. We have constructed the book to show that when we make disability justice a priority, we make life and society better for everyone. In this way, we have been greatly influenced by the scholarship of people such as Robert Chapman, who in *Empire of Normality* states that liberation for all is located in the development of a politics of neurodiversity and neurodivergent consciousness-raising. This is about developing a fluid understanding of who we all are in relation to capitalist systems of domination that are shaped by our material conditions, relations, and social practices.[12]

We use this introduction to begin to paint a picture of how we came to write this book together and the key scholarship and writings that guide the analysis in each chapter. As both a personal and a political intervention into the politics of neurodiversity, our objective has been to create an accessible yet rigorous discussion focused on social justice for everyone.

Friendship and Scholarship

We learned about our shared philosophy and vision of social justice very early on in our friendship. We met in 2018, when we both began working for Leading Routes, a pioneering organization founded by our sister Paulette Williams, designed to strengthen the academic pipeline for Black African and Caribbean students and staff in UK Higher Education (UKHE).[13] We instantly bonded over our shared experience of race and class and how difficult we had found education as neurodivergent children and adults. We also discovered that we had similar ways of coping; mitigating our own educational challenges through what can only be described as an obsession with helping others to reach their full potential in work and education. Part of this is about each of us having a spiritual pull towards the democratization of resources and redistribution of capital to people. But if we are honest and look a little more deeply, we can both see that it also comes from a position of wanting to determine our own places in a society in which our ways of being are so often deemed unworthy. How have we learnt to show we are of value? By being in service to others (see more in chapter 2 on the necessity of self-love).

As people from working class backgrounds, there was instant attunement and ease between us. We were early career academics when we met; our first conversation was mostly about education, money, and struggle. Chantelle was a part time PhD student with three paid jobs and family and healthcare responsibilities. Jason was a lecturer with multiple side hustles and jobs to help support his family and friends, a full-time carer for his parents, and a parent to his two children. In 2018 we were both employed and studying in universities, but even as early career academics it was natural that—on meeting someone with similar experiences of limited resources and access to capital—we voiced some of the difficulties we were facing. The social and cultural capital we have acquired through our education and jobs means we no longer consider ourselves to be working class (despite the fact that we still have to sell our labor to live!)

Of course, through industry and endeavor we are no longer working class, but that sense of permanent precarity and the memory of material struggle stays with you. In this way, our scholarly bond was first and foremost located in our class consciousness. We would later discover that alongside class consciousness was a spiritual, metaphysical, and neurodivergent connection that became fundamental to our ability to discuss what freedom might look like for the many. It is this connection that infuses each page of this book; it is something we see as a gift and a privilege, not to be taken for granted. When you meet siblings who have come to understand society through multiple lenses of marginalization, the possibilities are endless, not just because of similar experiences, but because we have understood those experiences in multiple ways across different settings and alongside a variety of people. Simply put, material, racialized, and classed similarity provide the grounds of a respectful union in which our differing ideas became grounded in ways that allowed us to learn, disagree, and grow in our thinking together.

While this collaborative project is about the politics of neurodiversity and neurotypical hegemony (see later sections of this chapter), we also feel that our dialogical and dialectical union demonstrates how building together with like-minded individuals is enhanced by similar lived experiences. This is a methodological intervention as well as a theoretical one, and it is imperative that the reader knows that a respectful union contains disagreement, debate, and conflict. For us, this is what love is. To produce work through the praxis of love is about recognizing and naming that love is seldom—in the seeds that are sown—about agreement alone. Love is about challenging and struggling through ideas and perspectives to produce a politics of emancipation. As bell hooks poignantly says, *it is the practice of love which transforms.*[14] Love transforms us and the world around us if engaged with in all of its beautiful, challenging, and painful dynamics.

Circling back, we know that we have been able to produce the book in this way because we have similar backgrounds. In times of angst, this has enabled us to locate familiarity as a tool to get back to each other. Human beings have a lot in common, and the only way to respect, collaborate, and learn together is through a loving framework of acceptance, discipline, and forgiveness. We do not claim to have all the answers, but we would like to think that our process of grappling with neurodiversity, disability, and society transcends a typical academic method of collaboration. We lean into our similarities through a loving praxis in order to learn, grow, and expand our ways of thinking and being.

At the same time, we are conscious that scholarly union, and even the political union of minds and experiences, have been used to uphold the inequitable social structures we seek to intellectually dismantle in this book. Though this is in no way a perfect science, we hope that readers will see how our ongoing awareness of critical friendship can contribute to the kind of liberalism we intend to expose and critiquee. As Noor and Shafee note, *"Generally, the roles of critical friends are to ask provocative questions, provide data to be examined through another lens, and offer a critique of a person's work as a friend."*[15] We have been guided by researchers who have worked in like-minded collectives or partnerships that have centered provocative questions and offered critique of a person's work. It is with this in mind that the political grounding of our relationship is one of revolution and transformation rather than reform. This is where we find it particularly useful to center teachings from fore parents such as bell hooks, who was clear that revolutionary feminism is about holistic self-actualization, which is embedded in dismantling an inequitable system.[16] Coming together through a shared belief system is not enough to make change. We need to challenge, disagree, and sit with our differences, too. As a Black mixed-race woman raised in the suburbs of the West Midlands, and a Black man from South London, it is natural that our distinctive experiences of early socialization (growing up) have in many instances produced perspectives on life and neurodiversity in each of us that differ from those held by the other.

As we delve more deeply into the political spirit of this book, it will become clear how our initial conversations about society back in 2018—alongside our love and respect for each other—foreground our arguments. While we weave sensitive, compassionate, and understanding threads of analysis throughout each chapter, the urgency of these times for social justice movements requires us to begin this book with a tone to match the political calamities we find ourselves in. Bear with us as—with some hard facts—in these introductory sections we set the scene for recognizing and taking seriously the politics of neurodiversity and disability for the twenty-first century.

Global Inequality

We write this book from the island of Britain and the United Kingdom. It is the summer of 2024, and this is currently one of the most inequitable countries in Europe and the World. According to the Equality Trust, the UK has a very high level of income inequality compared to other developed countries; crucially, wealth in Britain is even more unequally divided than income. In 2020, the Office for National Statistics (ONS) calculated that the richest ten percent of households owned forty-three percent of all wealth. The poorest fifty percent, by contrast, owned just nine percent.[17] After more than a decade of politically imposed austerity, there had been an increase in child poverty, systemic homelessness, a housing crisis, a huge wealth divide, and in many parts of the country social and public services often appeared to be in a state of collapse. In 2018, Philip Alston's United Nations envoy's report on poverty stated that the British government has inflicted "great misery" on its people with "punitive, mean-spirited, and often callous" austerity policies driven by a political desire to undertake social re-engineering rather than economic necessity.[18] In 2023, Olivier De Schutte, the UN's special rapporteur on extreme poverty and human rights, argued that poverty levels in the UK are "simply not acceptable" and that the government was violating international law.[19] In the USA, similar trends in economic and social inequality are being recorded, with Statista showing that in 2023, more than sixty-six percent of the total wealth was owned by the top ten percent of earners. In comparison, the bottom fifty percent of earners owned only a little over two and a half percent of the total wealth.[20] Moreover, according to the World Inequality Database, the richest ten percent in countries such as India, Maldives, and Thailand, earn more than half of the national income. Similarly, in Bangladesh, Nepal, and Singapore the richest ten percent earn about thirty–five percent of the national income. In a 2019 *American Economic Review* paper, Thomas Piketty, Li Yang, and Gabriel Zucman revealed that the top ten percent of the population of China holds approximately sixty-seven percent of its wealth and earns forty-one percent of the income. Meanwhile, the World Inequality Database shows that the continent of Africa suffers extreme levels of wealth inequality with the highest gap between the average incomes of the top ten percent and the incomes of the bottom fifty percent. The average incomes of the top ten percent are about thirty times higher than those of the bottom fifty percent, significantly higher than in other regions with extreme inequality.

We do not want these statements of fact to be read as in any way presentist; we understand the current system as part of a *longue durée* of constructed inequality sponsored by the legacies of colonialism, empire, and the extractive and profit driven cultures of capitalism. The key difference now is that there has never been this much absolute wealth alongside so much poverty and inequality. Leading scholars of social inequality, like Danny Dorling, contend that the global concentration of wealth persists because of the ongoing consensus that poverty is "natural."[21] This moment marks an emergency for the disabled community as these urgent political and social issues routinely marginalize physical and neurological minorities. These issues are an emergency for people who do not identify as disabled, too. The current lack of access to material, psychological, and structural care, support, and assistance is a multiclassed and multiethnic crisis; disabled people are simply at its sharpest end. As will be explored throughout the book, disability rights are integral to how we imagine dignity for all. People who do not identify as disabled are only ever one moment, one day or one year away from being at risk of marginalization via disability. This is about recognizing that our politics and how we understand humanity should always take into consideration our future selves and collectives, as well as our present-day disabled siblings. The social and political emergencies we find ourselves in have been informed by an ideological force focused on dehumanizing neurological and physical disabilities by way of ableism, racism, and capitalism. This is about recognizing that some lives have been deemed disposable. But in spite of this emphasis that "it could be you," we write this book in the spirit that love and empathy can be produced without the need to focus on readers' fears of becoming disabled themselves. What we hope is that the neurological and neurotypical majority will be able to see just how damaging this type of hegemony is for everyone, regardless of levels of individual risk.

We also write this book during a time of a widespread cultural complacency surrounding our thinking about the neurodiverse community. Committing to a revaluation of neurodiversity requires an unpacking of the way previous structures and institutions have contributed to some of the sustained misinterpretations of the disadvantage faced by neurodivergent people and families. Governments and stakeholders need to reflect on the practical consequences for the neurodivergent population, in particular the long-suffering parents and carers of neurodivergent people, who continue to be an afterthought. The structures put in place to ensure that resources are unattainable remain a stain on our society. The existing hierarchy situates disabled and neurodivergent people as disposable, with their contributions to civil society measured against the neurotypical hegemony that determines what and who is deemed to be of value.

Beyond Representation

While we pay close attention to how ableism is intrinsic to class inequality, we also look at what an increased representation of neurodiversity in the media means—tangibly—for the disability movement. In any given week, we find ourselves sending each other different media links detailing the variety of ways that neurodiversity is making the news. From celebrity diagnoses to women and ethnic minorities being given a platform to talk about their lived experience of race, gender, and disability—neurodiversity continues to present as a zeitgeist for these times. In Alice Wong's edited collection, *Disability Visibility: First-Person Stories from the Twenty-first Century,* it is clear that the shift in visibility afforded to disability and neurodivergence has been essential in bringing it from the margins to the center. Our recognition of the material politics of neurodiversity in the current context is aligned with our commentary on the cultures and discourse that surround this moment. Material politics here refers to the extent to which social and economic capital affect quality of life. Further, neurodiversity is a hot topic for people who take an interest in self-help and self-improvement resources, as well as more general discussions about how we as individuals manage and negotiate modern society. Naturally, people want to understand themselves. They want to understand how their personal and professional lives have been influenced by their neurodivergence and perhaps learn more about how to grapple with the challenges of living. We are witnessing a growth in formal diagnoses among women and ethnic minorities due to the structural implications of race, class, and gender in childhood.[22] These structures, which are fuelled by racism and sexism primarily, cause a delay in care that is only now being fully reconciled via adult diagnosis. And generally speaking, we observe this moment as a renewal of the capitalist cultures in which people want to delve more deeply into their sense of themselves to find solace in the face of the many extant political and environmental emergencies. Crucially, however, people are often being pushed to understand themselves in order to be better workers. But regardless of these critical ponderings on the discourse that surrounds neurodiversity, we come to the premise of this book as optimists. In spite of the—clearly much more sinister and capitalistic—cultures that are becoming established around neurodiversity, cultures that are often devoid of the radical roots of social justice movements, we remain convinced that if people could be provided with alternative ways of both understanding and communicating neurodivergence, this topic would have the capacity to be emancipatory for everyone, rather than simply being a trend.

Stretching our Imaginations

In-between our intensive writing sessions in Chantelle's kitchen or in Jason's native home of South London, we spent hours discussing the different ways of writing this book that would stretch our imaginations of neurodiversity (we'll come onto Frantz Fanon and stretching Marxism later in this chapter). We wanted to produce a resource that would go beyond the functioning of a single individual's brain. We wanted to create something that went beyond simply describing how the marginalization of neurodiversity could be resolved through the acts of individuals. But to go beyond individuality when we are working through a subject as fluid and diverse as neurodiversity is no easy feat. For starters, we needed to address the intensity of our feelings about the more universal marginalization of disabled people. We channel what Brittany Cooper conceptualizes as a Black women's feminist *eloquent rage* to guide us.[23] Being frustrated (and angry) about these cultures was a starting point; it gave us the passion and drive to articulate the problems. With this, when we first started to write this book, we often described feelings of isolation, ambivalence, and frustration when it came to thinking about which sorts of people are valued in society and the ways in which this is too-frequently mitigated by able-bodied-ness, neurotypical functioning, and mental health. What we have come to learn as we collaborate, research, and imagine together is that many of the scholars, activists, and freedom-fighters who have inspired us would perhaps today be understood as *disabled or neurodivergent*. Why is it that disability and neurodiversity are often understood in isolation or in terms of the experiences of specific individuals? Essentially, this is what frames the politics of this book; an emphasis on the movements and structures of society. By retrieving and centering the politics of neurodiversity as integral features of the formation of society, we are both resistant to and reliant on a politics that utilizes representation while recognizing that it can only ever be a starting point. The starting point for us in leaning on representative figures is very much about a sense of feeling, emotion, and connection. Put simply, seeing our experiences through the work of others makes us feel less alone. In later parts of the book—an essential feature of our critique of how neurodiversity is discussed—we highlight the toxic nature of neoliberalism. However, it would be disingenuous of us to state that the representation of neurodivergence by inspirational individuals did not move us. Although this book lays out a variety of critical interventions on neurodiversity, we are very clear that at the heart of our work is the human story. In this way, the voices and experiences of people who are like us inspire every page, and thus we explore what it means to be both critical and appreciative of the representation of neurodiversity and disability at this current moment.

Crucially, we write this book in admiration of the people who are sharing their stories of struggle in both childhood and adulthood as they try to manage their disabilities and neurodivergence in an increasingly ableist world. Fundamentally, we are seeing more conversations and more organizations that emphasize the strategies used by neurodivergent individuals to cope, adapt, and mask in everyday life.[24] When we were growing up in eighties, nineties, and noughties Britain as neurodivergent people, we could never have imagined this kind of representation, which not only validates our lived experiences of ableism, but gives a voice to various instances in each of our lives that are and have been specific and particular, and indeed deemed rather peculiar. Simply in seeing this new-found representation of neurodiversity outside societal structures, we feel an overwhelming warmth in the knowledge that future generations of neurodivergent people might see themselves presented as "ordinary." This ordinariness is the orthodoxy we want to promote, advance, and advocate for all, recognizing the importance attached to becoming a society that truly embraces intersectional differences in all their guises.

Introducing Neurotypical Hegemony

One of the most intriguing, yet possibly one of the more neurodivergent aspects of this book, is the fact that we rarely outline or discuss the specificity of living with neurodivergent traits in isolation. Our focus is mainly on the proliferation of neurotypical culture (domination and power), in a move to collectivize the politics of neurodiversity. This is of course inspired by the movement of critical disabilities scholars who have dedicated much of their careers to recognizing the extent to which our points of entry into structural inequity can be enhanced by an intentional engagement with disability, affect, and society (see for example Therí A. Pickens, Dan Goodley, Kirsty Liddiard and Katherine Runswick-Cole, Rebecca Lawthom, Anna Hinton, Sami Schalk and Robert McRuer). This is about recognizing how our sense of self is constructed in relation to how we have been and continue to be affected both emotionally and structurally by the way society is organized. With this, we see that looking closely at how normative (or "normal") ideas become so intensely valued provides a route into the ongoing, yet incredibly important, work of addressing the conflict, connection, and challenge of both structure and agency. Rather, scholars such as Goodley, Liddiard, and Runswick-Cole note that the intersection of disability shows that, for the disabled community, the interaction between the relational, the political, and the social cuts across a variety of issues at the forefront of matters that are both queer and feminist.[25] We take many of these guiding principles into our contribution to the field to show that *different ways of knowing and experiencing the world* are often thwarted by the constraints of neurotypical society. In this way, we bring the politics of neurodiversity into consistent conversation with the primary concept we use throughout this book—*neurotypical hegemony*.

Neurotypical hegemony gets its own section in our introduction because it forms the basis of our critical overview of the best ways to embrace neurodivergence and generate hopeful and inclusive futures for all. Firstly, we break down the term in two distinct ways. "Neurotypical" describes the neurological majority whose modes of thinking, being, and living have become embedded in society; neurotypical people are seen as the normal, most valuable, and valued citizens. Scholars of neurodiversity, such as Dieuwertje Dyi Huijg, note that the connection between agency (or how the structured position of a person affects the way they interact with their environment) and "normality" is grounded in "neuronormativity." This process systematically represents neurotypical minds as being the "normal state."[26] The word neurotypical represents both people and culture and is used throughout our analysis as the central phenomenon we are trying to disrupt and dismantle. Neurotypical hegemony means cultural and social dominance. As sociologists, our overview of neurotypicality resists individualizing the harm it inflicts, avoiding a politics of "good" and "bad," and instead situating it as both tied to and socially reproduced through a combination of structures. In this way, both the neuromajority and the neurominority support and protect neurotypical culture, which has been conveyed routinely as the only safe and viable way for society to be organized. Put simply, neurotypical culture has become so powerful because it is able to dominate even through the actions and ideas of the people and communities it consistently marginalizes.

To complete our account of the term neurotypical culture as something ideologically entrenched and powerful, we use the humanist Marxist term hegemony. Humanist Marxism is attentive to the ways that capitalism becomes socially reproduced through the power of ideas and values. We use the framework of civil society as responsive to the notion that society is intentionally curated through the guise of the "most tolerated citizen." This is achieved through a combination of common sense (or how ideas and values become described and positioned as normal and normative), and consent (or how people and society give permission for certain cultures to dominate). We will now take a brief but crucial introductory historical detour to the concept of hegemony, to lay the foundations for the way we use the term throughout the book.

Gramsci, Hegemony, and Modern Society

The concept of hegemony was first developed by Antonio Gramsci, when he was General Secretary of the Italian Communist Party, during his years in prison (1926–1935). In *Quaderni del Carcere* (*The Prison Notebooks*), Gramsci established the basic premise of the theory of hegemony in a series of dispersed writings which, in the simplest terms, argued that power is concealed, consented to, and socially reproduced by a range of social agents (people!).[27] Thus, hegemony means both power and dominance. It is achieved through the combination of "civil society" and "common sense" and becomes a social contract. To deviate from its cultures is to become a challenging citizen or member of civil society. This contextualized focus on hegemony is a way of emphasizing how it becomes normalized, naturalized, and also struggled over, both intimately and socially. For Gramsci, the state is the base on which political power is woven, through the production of ideas and values. With this power, the terrain is set for how these cultures present in "civil society." Civil society is maintained by the ways in which media, education, and religious institutions (primarily) become integral to the formation of people's identities, which ultimately contribute to the conditioning of the ideological power that regulates ideas, values, and social norms. The sphere of civil society is where hegemony operates, negating the need for coercive control; it requires ongoing investment in the protection and reproduction of the ideologies that preserve power.

A closer look at what Gramsci calls *common sense* provides us with some key sites of everyday life which can help introduce just how integral hegemony is for the social reproduction of ideas and the values we all live by. For the purpose of laying the foundations of a world seen through the lens of neurotypical hegemony we see how schools, politicians, the media, and pop culture become integral components in the creation of principles that are simultaneously both common sense and marginalizing, such as ableism, racism, and capitalism. In the context of the politics of neurodiversity, this means that neurodivergence becomes marginal simply because key social institutions have committed to cultures that understand disability as a phenomenon synonymous with inferiority. Each institution in civil society relies on the others to reproduce common sense in this way. An example of this in the context of neurodiversity and disability is the combined existence of austerity alongside pupil referral units (the removal of young people from mainstream school), and the repeated recommissioning of *The Undateables* on Channel Four (which has to date run for eleven series).[28] Each institution commits to a pathologization of neurodiversity and disability through common sense notions of the normality of social and economic marginalization. This becomes most dangerous in the social reproduction of consent, which is where hegemony creates its winning formula. For humanist Marxists and especially for Gramsci, hegemony is most dangerous where it is seen to be winning on multiple fronts. Consent across key social institutions enables the dehumanizing of populations that are rarely at the forefront of creating the power required for ideological control. Keeping in mind TV shows like *The Undateables* and *Love on the Spectrum*,[29] our concern is with the ways in which material and social marginalization can exist while also being presented as entertainment. In its most sinister form, the combination of consent and common sense produces a hegemonic condition where those who are most likely to be marginalized in civil society portray this ideological culture as reasonable. Simply put, hegemony's appeal for the most powerful is that it allows them to control ideas about populations they see as disposable, and they can win even the minds of the people at the sharper end of this culture. As Marx said, the proletariat experiences the constant suppression of a sense of self alongside the structural insecurity that has been fed to them as integral to their survival. If societal cultures—and hegemony—work hard enough, they can convince those positioned by them as least valuable that their position is well-founded.

It is in these foundations of hegemony that we see the clear connection between the ways in which neurodiversity and disability become understood as marginal, and the way that neurodiverse and disabled people are positioned as the opposite of the most valuable, valued, and loveable citizens (see chapters 2 and 3).

Love and Political Education

We contend throughout this book that exploring the way neurotypical hegemony persists provides the information required to produce more loving ways to live with and relate to each other. We present this information to demonstrate the utopian possibilities of political education, in the understanding that *knowledge is power*. Throughout our themed discussions, from subjects like mental health to schooling and class, we stress that *we only know what we know,* and sometimes it is only by exploring these matters through anecdotes and by relating issues to each other that we can truly understand their interconnection. We are guided by many scholars, but in particular by Black feminist educators such as Patricia Hill Collins, who notes that political education and knowledge production more broadly are rooted in a consciousness-raising which fuels individual and collective empowerment to change and revolutionize how we live and relate to each other.[30] Learning about the histories of

how, as people and collectives, we have experienced life in relation to the structures of society forms the basis for the liberatory politics found in this book. On the essential *practice of
knowing* how society is constructed through its ableist, racist,
and capitalist tendencies, global commentaries from Black
feminists over the past fifty years help to prompt some of our
more poignant critiques throughout this book. An example of
the importance of political education as we negotiate a society
fixated on obscuring consciousness-raising can be found among
our Black British feminist siblings, such as Lola Young, Beverley
Bryan, Stella Dadzie and Suzanne Scafe, Gail Lewis, Elizabeth
Obi, Olive Morris, Marsha Prescod, Lauretta G. Ngcobo, Julia
Chinyere Oparah (previously Sudbury) and many more.[31]
Among these writers and activists, many of those located on the
island we currently find ourselves writing from have been committed to documenting the lived experiences of racialized and
gendered struggle as a way of surviving a society fixated on
making inequality invisible. Though there is no doubt that
the digital and technological revolution has produced more
fertile ground for political education, the activity of concealing
the lives of those who find themselves in some of the darkest
and most helpless places in contemporary society persists.[32] As
Tracey Reynolds has noted, the limited and limiting representations of how contemporary inequality is rooted in its historical
constructions show just how radical the Black feminist tradition of telling stories from the standpoint of knowing has been
for other movements for social justice.[33] In this way, political
education rooted in existing resistance to the media, government, and civil society more broadly provides space for us to
use the democratization of information as a vehicle for generating cultures of love and understanding. Knowing who we are
and how society is co-produced is where Black feminists have

so often found the possibilities for liberatory politics. We take up this baton to enhance our commitment to exposing neurotypical hegemony; doing so is one of the ways love is connected to political education. If we do not commit to understanding ourselves and others non-judgmentally via historical formations, then we will continue to produce lovelessness. It is this philosophy of love, rooted in awareness of the systemic nature of multiple processes of harms, to which bell hooks so poignantly suggested we must commit. hooks was clear that we must understand ourselves in relation to others, in addition to recognizing the harms that fall outside our control. Put simply, unless we commit to recognizing multiple sites of inequity, then we will routinely act in self-interested ways in an effort to end only that which harms us personally.[34]

We have been privileged to have the time and space to think, read, and reflect together about how we can best interpret the persistence of neurotypical hegemony, and the discussions in this book form part of our civic duty to bring these ideas together to help everyone make sense of inequity and the kinds of knowledge required for emancipation for all. By explicitly exploring the various ways in which social life is constrained by neurotypical hegemony, we can generate alternative ways of living that are embedded in a love of all people. It is only by being abundantly clear about the ways neurotypical hegemony is constructed that we can we work out how to truly dismantle its power and imagine alternative ways of understanding difference. Inevitably, there will be critics of our approach who might be at odds with our method, which seeks to expose inequity in order to manifest visions of equity for all. Some might suggest that taking this holistic stance as a route to the production of a loving epistemology of neurodiversity is overly simplistic. In response, we want to highlight the embedded nature of neurotypical hegemony and the ableist emergencies we are currently living through. It is only by explicitly recognizing the everyday and taken-for-granted nature of ableism that we can find the language and tools to move beyond it.

Throughout the book, we stress that political education provides routes to addressing the interconnection between ableism, racism, and capitalism and their reliance on the social reproduction of neurotypical hegemony. This is primarily achieved by making visible a fusion of the concepts of neurotypical culture and hegemony that can help us communicate in transparent ways the extent to which this process is integral to multiple sites of marginalization and oppression. Once we have named these matters across civil society, we can better communicate ways of *getting back to love*. In this way, transparency becomes an emblem of hope for the arguments. The ability to access information is at the same time where hope lies, *and* what needs to be democratized. The optimists in us believe that if people had a more thorough understanding of how neurotypical hegemony and ableism persist, they would be more likely to question them. Our hope lies in the power of knowledge and the interconnection of struggles for ordinary and dignified lives.

Black Subjectivities and Afterlives

We write this book through the lens of our Black and neurodivergent subjectivities, which have been shaped by colonial and postcolonial historical and contemporary formations of society.[35] Subjectivity in this sense refers to how our personal feelings and emotions become constructed through our view of ourselves and the world around us. As sociologists, we see our experiences of observing society as intrinsic to how we come to understand ourselves and our value (see chapter 6, on value).

As much as many of us would like to contend that our minds are separate entities that operate on the basis of the facts to hand, we are all highly influenced by our social environments and the changing nature of civil society. While we rely on a variety of visions for social justice that cut across critical disability studies, Black feminism, and class analysis, our starting point for much of this work has been informed by our position as Black (British) people who have taken solace in analyzing our position in society, emphasizing the long-term impact of British colonialism in particular, as well as the transatlantic slave trade and its afterlives. Put simply, we are residing in the afterlife of the British empire, in which we are witnessing a deeply personal, political, and structural process of decolonization.[36] As much as we strive to free ourselves from categories of difference such as race and disability, how we see ourselves and how others view us continues to be influenced by the society we find ourselves in. As Matthew Lange notes, on the breadth and extent of the British empire:

> While recognizing that the British were neither the creators nor the sole colonizers employing indirect forms of rule, British colonialism was exceptional in at least one aspect— namely the size and diversity of the British Empire, which caused Great Britain to rely much more extensively on both direct and indirect modes of domination than any other colonial power.[37]

In the face of Britain's colonization of around thirty-three nations, and its creation of further settler colonies in Australia, Canada, New Zealand, South Africa, and the United States, the process of decolonization of the British Empire requires the close attention of anyone attempting to produce an analysis of visions for social justice, simply because of the scale of

influence and domination we are seeking to unravel. Frantz
Fanon, a psychiatrist who played an active role in the Algerian
War for independence from French colonial rule, is a key
thinker to whom we return throughout this book as we strive
to incorporate the way histories of colonialism and struggles for
independence among oppressed groups can help generate dialects and practices for dismantling neurotypical hegemony. As
we contend in both chapters 2 (Love) and 3 (Mental Illness),
neurotypical hegemony relies on a variety of accomplices acquired through the historical formations of ableism, racism, and
capitalism. As authors, we are living embodiments of these tensions and continue to see how Fanon's conception of the *colonial world* is reflected in our subjectivity as well as that of many
other people.[38] We see the legacies of the ongoing encounter
between European colonial settlers and native populations, defined and sustained by violence, as integral to any modern
analysis of inequality. Writing from the home front (Britain) of
a country that at one point had the greatest colonial and imperialist reach, we see the historical degradation of our ancestors,
between Africa and the Caribbean in particular, as continuing
to inform the postcolonial conditions of contemporary society.
According to Fanon, there was a dual process of colonial domination. Firstly, ideas of Western democracy became subverted
by the proliferation of racist and scientific theories about native
populations that were concentrated in the psyche of the colo-
nizers (the British). The second part of this dual process was
the internalization of dehumanizing and violent colonial relations to impede and destroy a sense of self, due to "a belief in
fatality [which] removes all blame from the oppressor."[39] To
this day, this thwarting, doubting, and constraining limits the
range of motion that Black and indigenous people have to move
towards an evolved sense of self. For Black people more

generally, their sense of self is still significantly constrained through histories of domination, racism, and subordination.[40]

These tensions are alive and well both locally and globally as we write this book. When we assert the importance of confirming our Black subjectivity, we are informed by the ongoing violence and harms to which our siblings have been subjected, which was evidently grounded in the formation of the colonial world. Here in the UK, Black people are nine times more likely to be stopped and searched by police than white people.[41] Black women are four times more likely to die in childbirth. They are twice as likely to experience stillbirth and baby death as white women and are at higher risk of having an early birth and a baby with low birthweight.[42] Across the UK, more people from Black, Asian, and other minority ethnic backgrounds are likely to be in poverty (i.e., have an income less than sixty percent of the average household income) than white British people. In 2020, the Social Metrics Commission found that nearly half (forty-six percent, or 900,000 people) of all people living in families where the household head was Black/African/Caribbean/Black British were in poverty, compared to just under one in five (nineteen percent) of those living in families where the head of household was white. In 2022, an analysis by the Runnymede Trust found that Black and Minority Ethnic people are two and a half times more likely to be in relative poverty (individuals who have an income below sixty percent of the median) and more than twice as likely to live in deep poverty (an income more than fifty percent below the relative poverty line).[43] In early 2023, the United Nations wrote to the UK government to express "very extreme concern" about its failure to address "structural, institutional and systemic racism" against people of African descent in Britain.[44] The postcolonial afterlives of Black people haunt contemporary society, something that informs how we come to write, communicate, and expose all aspects of inequity. Without an emphasis on Black subjectivity we would hardly complete an analysis true to the social reproduction of neurotypical hegemony. As we will stress throughout this book, understanding the connection between neurodivergence and the negative racialization of Black people in particular can help to develop a universal vision of freedom for all.

We have already begun to formulate some of these ideas around Black subjectivity, postcolonial afterlives and neurodiversity in an article about sociology's complicity in the social reproduction of neurotypical hegemony.[45] But this tension between the oppressor and the self, as a product of histories of colonial domination, is something we see as integral to the starting point of our analysis of the multifaceted ways that neurotypical hegemony obstructs the entirety of society.

Black Studies and Marxism

This is a book about how neurotypical ways of creating a society marginalize *all* people. We emphasize *all* people to make clear that for us there are no winners in a neurotypical society. There are those who feel and experience our cultures more intensely, but our arguments more broadly stress the fact that the norms and values (and policies) that have embedded neurotypical culture as normal are in fact harming everyone. In this way, our work in this book bridges multiple modes of thinking and imagines a more equitable and utopian society for all, through a fusion of Black studies by way of Black feminism, Marxism, and critical disability studies. All these schools of thought are formed through the subjectivity of people who have a historical and contemporary understanding of marginality that breaches a variety of intersections. This provides a viewpoint from which to see the roots of some of society's biggest inequalities. Black and disabled people have combined experience of racism, classism, and ableism that creates a unique yet informative experience of society that can generate utopian visions for a range of people and populations.

Black studies' influence on the theoretical and practical application of knowledge production is incorporated throughout our discussion. In this way, the democratization of education and knowledge is grounded by our reading of Fanon and his practice of stretching Marxism as a way to incorporate the impact of the colonial world and account for the racial subjugation of colonized people. This is about understanding how class equity relies on the historical formations of colonial capitalism. It is not enough to simply state that there are two classes—the owners of the means of production and the workers.[46] The impact of the ruling classes on workers and the uneven distribution of wealth cannot be adequately addressed without recognizing the inextricable link between colonialism, capitalism, and racism. The integral nature of race and class in developing an analysis of the dominance of neurotypical hegemony relies on the histories of capitalism as shaped by ideas, people, and values.

Returning to the influence of Gramsci and the conception of hegemony we use throughout this book, we see how the fusion of our Black subjectivity with neurodivergence can symbolize existing movements of both the Black radical tradition and disability justice more broadly. Taking a closer look at the personhood of Gramsci himself, we see a man who self-described as experiencing a *constant worm within his brain*. While he was incarcerated, Gramsci wrote about neurological difference, disability, and poor mental health. Some of his earliest writings as a young man show the way he understood his brain and how it differed from others. What this tells us in the first instance is that it can be useful to retrace the lives of intellectuals to unearth their experience of, or proximity to, disability. Paying attention to the scholars behind the theories allows us to demonstrate ways of highlighting the prominence of disability in shaping liberatory ideas. If we understand people and movements as routinely embodying disability rights, the next step is to name the way both disability and neurodiversity are always already in the ether of social justice. Part of our work is about naming this, but our contentions throughout the book are fundamentally centered around imagining equity between all bodies and minds, and exposing the ways neurotypical hegemony infringes upon freedom. The societal restriction imposed on the neurodiverse community has involved a chastising and a minimizing of intellectual capability. This has usually involved framing consideration and discussions of disability within a perception of enduring deficit. Importantly, there is a celebration of difference that straddles the intersection, allowing us to have more mature conversations about what is needed to create a society that can better adapt to the needs of the neurodiverse community.

The Chapters: Ableism, Racism, and Capitalism

The key concepts that bind and connect our arguments in this book around the harms caused by neurotypical hegemony to all people are ableism, racism, and capitalism. Our intentions here are to stress that these are the key principles of neurotypical hegemony and it is only by intentionally making clear their historical and contemporary formations that we can bring together a variety of overlapping and connected struggles. Our presentation of both ableism and racism is embedded in both their interpersonal (between groups and individuals) and institutional occurrences. Ableism is rooted in the assumption that typical abilities are superior and that disabled people require "fixing." Generally speaking, it is the constant prioritization of the needs of people who do not identify as disabled over the needs of others. For Fiona Kumari Campbell, ableism is a "network of beliefs, processes and practices that produces a particular kind of self and body (the corporeal standard) that is projected as the perfect, species-typical and therefore essential and fully human."[47] For us, as Black neurodivergent people, the connection between ableism and racism in particular can be found in who is seen as deserving of value. Which groups or types of people are considered to be human or worthy of human status has always been historically contentious. In Katherine McKittrick's edited collection *Sylvia Wynter: On Being Human as Praxis*, the variety of essays that speak to Sylvia Wynter's interpretation of humanness helped us to see ourselves and other as products of a social history that has constantly changed, moved, and evolved the parameters of humanness and ordinariness. Crucially, this sorting of people is constantly found to be informed by ableist and racist values, beliefs, policies, and institutions. In this way, to ground our use of "racism," we look firstly at "race," taking inspiration from scholars such as Alana Lentin, who in her book, *Why Race Still Matters*, asserts that race should be understood as a technology of power.

> I formulate race as a technology for the management of human difference, the main goal of which is the production, reproduction, and maintenance of White supremacy on both a local and a planetary scale.[48]

The concept of race as a technology of power helped us to connect the ways in which the above process overlaps with— and consequently attend to the tensions and connections between—ableism, racism, and later capitalism. Racism is what Ruth Wilson Gilmore defined in the *Golden Gulag* as "the state-sanctioned or extralegal production and exploitation of group-differentiated vulnerability to premature death."[49] Racism is the process by which systems and policies, actions and attitudes create inequitable opportunities and outcomes for people based on race. Racism is about history and how it can impact different communities in different ways in the present day. The connection of neurodivergence and disability to racism and ableism which you will find across each chapter of this book is in how these social processes are linked to productivity, value, and disposability. Simply put, humanness is defined as those who are able to participate in civil society in a way that is not seen to disrupt the production of capital, wealth, land, and resources.

In our exploration of subjects related to love, work, education, and mental illness (to name a few), we return to ableism, racism, and capital as a way to build solidarity across difference and do the messy work of joining up our struggles for more ordinary and dignified lives. Throughout, in putting together our arguments, narratives, and provocations we feel it is important to continue to make clear that this intervention should be understood as one that builds on the work of many others. In this way, we make this small contribution to the large swathes of work, research, and scholarship that came before us, while also wishing to make clear that we are not able to cover all the pressing and urgent matters related to disability justice or other urgent movements such as global emergencies related to land, space, and climate.

The book is organized into seven key chapters, along with an eighth, which we have called our Afterword. In chapter 2 we demonstrate how we have used both our Black subjectivity and love, in theory and practice, to write this book. We stress the need for the politics of neurodiversity to be embedded in loving frameworks of analysis which take seriously race and class, self-love and self-actualization. In this slightly longer chapter, we also draw on the Black feminist literature and methodology which guided our approach to writing this book. In chapter 3 we look at the more individualized harms of mental illness and health that are caused by neurotypical hegemony, with the help of crucial (and critical) disabilities research and the movement more generally. In chapter 4 we are looking at the institution of education as key to highlighting how neurotypical hegemony persists in our understanding of "achievement." In chapter 5, we give time to the inextricable links and connections between neurodiversity and race and class. In chapter 6 we look at how value is produced, and how it creates hierarchies of "worthiness." In our conclusion (chapter 7), we have created an eleven-point manifesto in which we provide practical points to consider for dismantling neurotypical hegemony. Finally, in chapter 8 we platform the British scandal of the Educationally Subnormal Schools and the need for the psychological research communities and the public more broadly to recognize this as a key part of understanding the histories of the disability justice movement.

Thank you for joining us on this journey.

2

What's Love Got to Do with It?

A FRAMEWORK OF LOVE TO DISMANTLE NEUROTYPICAL HEGEMONY

I've been takin' on a new direction
But I have to say
I've been thinkin' about my own protection
It scares me to feel this way

(TINA TURNER, 1984)

KNOWN FOR her rawness, magnetism, authenticity, and passion, Tina Turner (in our eyes as well as those of many others) holds the mantle of the queen of rock'n'roll. The lyrics and title of this chapter are from Turner's 1984 single—"What's Love Got to Do with It?"—a passionate rock'n'roll ballad infused with the beautiful yet challenging emotions that romantic love has the capacity to produce. It was written by Graham Lyle and Terry Britten and recorded for Turner's fifth studio album, *Private Dancer* (1984). Later to become Turner's biggest-selling single, "What's Love Got to Do with It?" forms the introductory reflections for this chapter. Our interpretation of the song is one that contains an appreciation of the provocations and revelations that love unleashes across society and our relationships. Though Turner's breath-taking vocals are largely understood as discussing the pain associated with romantic love, we see this song as demonstrating how lovelessness in society becomes connected to our sense of self—we see unloving feelings as inextricably linked to the structures that decide what sort of people are deemed to be of value. We position love as the question, the answer, and the direction. Love in this way has *everything to do with it*. It is how we meet each other where we are; how we understand ourselves and our histories and how we all get free. Understanding love as a way of living and relating to our world, and as a practice that transcends romantic love, we turn to the lyrics from the title of this chapter, such as *"who needs a heart when a heart can be broken,"* as a way of drawing out and naming our fears and projections about society. We all need the framework and practice of love as a way to avert brokenness, as a means to enlightenment, acceptance, and peace.

The introductory reflections above provide us with the direction of this chapter, which outlines the theoretical and methodological commitment and processes found throughout this book. As we wrote in chapter 1, we have chosen to lean on our siblings in Black studies by way of Black feminism, Marxist thought, and critical disability studies to help us dismantle neurotypical hegemony. The overall objective of this chapter is to demonstrate how an emphasis on love with the politics of neurodiversity, alongside a critical exploration of neurotypical hegemony, can generate conversations and practices for all social justice movements. In this way, we show how Black feminist interventions concerned with the way our (Black) lived experiences and (neurodivergent) personal troubles become incorporated into strategies of resistance through social research and knowledge production for the whole of society. In this chapter, we present our loving frame of analysis, which will read as the "backstory," narrating how lovelessness and a lack of love becomes synonymous with neurotypical hegemony.

Once we have set out the grounding of love, we outline our theoretical direction, which we argue is a fusion between humanist Marxism and Black feminism. We understand the social construction of civil society as an ideological tool integral to the maintenance of neurotypical hegemony. We remind readers exactly how we are using the concept of hegemony, based on our discussion in chapter 1, and make clear how the combination of Black subjectivity, consent, and common sense provides the theoretical grounds for the whole book, which gives us a route to dismantling the cultures we see as integral to the combination of ableism, racism, and capitalism.

The chapter is divided into three sections that establish our commitment to explaining our interpretation of the politics of neurodiversity and neurotypical hegemony through a combination of theory and practice. First, we explain exactly how we are applying a loving framework—or a theory of love—throughout this book, as well as ways to both expose and dismantle neurotypical hegemony. We believe that in order to really get to grips with the radical potential of love, we have to explain exactly how our use of the term goes beyond more traditional understandings of love of the romantic or parental types. In order to understand and accept the multitude of ways it can be exercised, we position love throughout this book as an intentional practice. We align this intervention with bell hooks' note that more popular depictions of relationships, such as romantic love, can sometimes disguise the more fluid and emancipatory possibilities of love and genuine love. In the novel, *The Bluest Eye*, Toni

Morrison went as far as describing the concept of "romance" or romantic love as one of the most destructive ideas in human thought.[1] Though it is not our intention to critique romantic love, we do appreciate and take seriously how misconceptions about the truly expansive nature of love can detract from our experience and enacting of its emancipatory possibilities.

Finally, we lay out our methodological process. We used Black feminist thought as method while writing the book. Part of our commitment to being transparent about collaborative and neurodivergent means of production is to contribute to a culture that expands the way we view knowledge. We call this "neurodivergent sociology," which draws on the same iterative, interactive, and collaborative ways of working we use. This section of the discussion combines celebration with caution about what it means to work, produce, and create with people with whom we broadly agree about most aspects of social life. Celebration refers to the emancipatory possibilities of critical friendship, while recognizing the limitations of what has at times been described as a liberal process of agreement—or backing ourselves via strength in numbers. The reasons for stressing caution include recognizing the more general issues that affect knowledge production, as well as the importance of reflexivity. As a framework to explore how we bridge the theoretical and practical elements of this book methodologically, we draw on Patricia Hill Collins' four dimensions of Afrocentric feminist epistemology: (a) lived experience as a criterion of meaning, (b) the use of dialogue to assess knowledge claims, (c) the ethics of caring, and (d) the ethics of personal accountability.[2] We finish the section and this chapter by exploring how our multisensory ways of communicating have enabled us to better understand intimate, social, and structural engagements *in and with society.*

Structure, Agency, and Love

Love is about creating structural and interpersonal cultures which generate the conditions for people to live ordinary and dignified lives. As Black scholars primarily disciplined within sociology, we feel it is important to explain how we arrived at a theory of love through our ongoing and continuous examination of the tension between structure and agency. Our perspective on love and its relationship to the politics of neurodiversity and life itself is of course embedded in and influenced by our lived experience of society and relationships. Structure is how society becomes socially reproduced through race, class, and gender, and how these become embedded in institutions deemed integral to the life course such as the family, education, health, government, and media. Agency refers to people, the self, and the individual. We see our relationships as produced through both structure and agency. This is sociology-speak for the fact that society and people co-create their own lives and the trajectories they follow. These reflections are of course inspired by both our critiques and our appreciation of our sociological fore parents, such as Alexander, on "structure, order and life chances" or Durkheim on social reality *sui generis* (when individual consciences interact and fuse together to create an inimitable reality), or of course, Giddens' emphasis on structure and agency as in "dialectical interplay," between individual action and social order in specific situational contexts.[3] All these theorists were concerned with how we make the society we live in and how our active making of society affects the way it is made. The early stages of this process can be found in the ways that the structures we are born into—like poverty or wealth—affect how we view society, how we are guided to engage in it as infants and how we choose to engage as adults. This tension, which so many of us sociology enthusiasts are concerned with, shapes how we view individuality. Positioning people outside the structures through which they have come to live and understand themselves only tells a fraction of the story. And when it comes to the politics of neurodiversity discussed throughout this book, we see the limitations of individuality as integral to our ongoing resistance to exploring the neurodivergent person in isolation from the structures and collectives through which we have come to understand ourselves. Put simply, the self and the structure are combined; looking at the dominating cultures around us is a way to better frame and understand who we are and who we become.

When we began thinking about how we could contribute to a more universal sociological discussion of neurodiversity and disability, we reflected a lot on the individualized nature of neurodivergence, while we pondered how could we adequately imagine social justice for everyone if our society so often moderates our access to love through historical and existing social structures. The structures we are referring to here primarily concern the institutions and cultures that are socially reproduced in civil society. An example could be the way the education system has become stratified by intersections of race, class, and gender. In schools, this means groups of young people become predisposed to being understood, organized, and received in relation to the historical and contemporary formations of society. Later in the book, we describe these processes as they are exemplified though the cultural and social reproduction of the institution of education (see chapter 4). Agency refers to the various moments at which individuals respond to and are affected by the formulation of these structures around us. Agency is about an individual's active response to the structures they find themselves negotiating. We see the possibilities of transcending these tensions in the recognition—noted by scholars such as Margaret Archer—that neither structure nor agency necessarily determine societal outcomes.[4] Structure remains integral but hope can be found through an emphasis *on agents within their collectives.* This is what social justice movements like the emergence of the neurodiversity paradigm have shown—self-actualization through resistance to deficit language around disability alongside a critical depiction of the ableist cultures structures produce.[5] This is about how society is organized, which requires an intentional process of living and learning in tandem. This is coupled with an ongoing look at ourselves in relation to others, not as a means to develop hierarchies of pain and struggle, but more to find solidarities that transcend difference and ways to commit to soft forms of advocacy for everyone in our everyday lives. This outer work (how we see others and how we see ourselves in relation to others) on understanding society informs the inner work (how we see ourselves), which we see as fundamentally connected to how we imagine and create loving cultures as ordinary. Again, these are tensions, and our reflections here follow routes that prioritize love alongside a recognition that neurotypical hegemony produces cultures (and structures) that damage every aspect of society. Structures are what produce cultures of lovelessness. The more we see and name them, the closer we come to an enlightened understanding of neurological difference.

Part of our work in this book is about recognizing that structures of inequality have a fundamental impact on a person's life and sense of self and that this process is intensified by neurotypical hegemony. While our critiques of the social reproduction of racism, ableism, and capitalism are clear, our arguments are also made in the recognition that people do have agency and that there are choices we can make in relation to the structures of society that could produce change and evolution in our worlds. Public intellectuals such as Brené Brown have produced many books on these matters; her podcast specifically uncovers different themes in relation to building core values around our sense of self that resist the structures around us.[6] Returning to the self is something we do throughout our reflections in this book. But with this, the challenge is still the challenge, and walking through it with the help of neurodivergent perspectives can really make a difference to how we tackle structure and agency with love. We contend that it is the tensions surrounding structure and individuality that can begin to demonstrate the challenge for producing intentionally loving cultures for all people. Taking seriously the affective turn and the scholarly contribution of Black feminists throughout our discussions is about generating a praxis of love that connects the practical, emotional, and challenging dichotomies that structure and agency provide. This is about naming what bell hooks calls "talking back" on just how much these tensions impact our lives and how unevenly distributed they are. How we interact with structure creates a surplus of responses that at times can lead us away from an acceptance of others and their differing paths. Social theorists concerned with how society and structures inform our sense of self, such as Judith Butler, contend that living socially means, by and large, that we are putting our lives in the hands of others and how they will receive us.[7] Here, we recognize the existence of a huge number of variables surrounding how we live, as well as the fact that other people's agency and interactions with structure also affect our own lives. We write about these tensions from a place of understanding too; for so many people, structure has been a source of pain and anguish, so to step into love when living through such a pressurized situation can be incredibly challenging. Here, we need look no further than the global populations of parents and carers who have dedicated their lives to creating dignified and fulfilling experiences for their disabled and neurodiverse family and community members. Of course, to stress that the answer is love could—among the pressures that neurotypical hegemony produces alongside existing formations of racism, ableism, and capitalism—be taken as a flimsy response to these cultures. For this reason, we reconcile with this challenge by taking seriously the idea that the ways in which society is structured can thwart the radical possibilities of love.

In an interview with Nasar Meer in 2016 for the British Sociological Association's flagship journal *Sociology*, John Holmwood reflected on the contemporary disconnect among social scientists regarding the tension between structure and agency. He noted that the division between those who see the self as socially formed "through the nature of the social and its structures . . . [and] as crucial in determining out-comes and life chances" is still primarily in opposition to the behavioral scientists who see "the self as a product of inheritance and environment in early years."[8] While we are of course sympathetic to Holmwood's notes on the former, we see the combination of these two camps as crucial to a more contemporary analysis of structure and agency, especially when considering love and the politics of neurodiversity. We have in mind the work of the radical thinker and physician, Gabor Maté, who has consistently confirmed—in his research on neurodiversity, trauma, and addiction—that the emotional environment of a person's early years is crucial to an understanding of self.[9] Specifically, traumatic experiences, including neglect, abuse, or even subtle emotional distress, can be pivotal. And of course, this is a class politics. The traumatic experience of a child whose family lives in acute poverty must be understood as fundamentally different from the experience of a privately educated, materially and financially well-resourced, child. The key difference between them is the potential opportunity or 'agency' the child might have to access the care required to heal and recover from harm.

As we look closely at how neurotypical hegemony becomes socially reproduced, we see how the institutions of civil society interact with the self from a very early age. These interactions are often mitigated by the experiences of parents, carers, teachers, and peers, who themselves have spent much of their lives negotiating the impact of institutions on their agency (the way that institutions such as school and the family affect how people see themselves). In modern society, we know that many families experience an ongoing battle for equitable teaching and learning spaces for children with special educational needs, as well as disabled and neurodivergent children. We know that access to capital and resources has become a fundamental component of who gets access to space to fulfil their passions in both education and work (see chapter 5). To begin to address the task at hand, we remind the reader of the cyclical nature of structure and agency when it comes to producing new patterns of living with and through love. Those who have greater resources (mainly financial) and support (care-givers and friends with time and space to help them negotiate life's ups and downs) are likely to have a more linear relationship with a creatively fulfilled life. The cyclical nature is that by and large, this process (or privilege) is often inherited.

On the importance of structure and its relationship to the development of individual agency, Karl Marx stated that "people make their own history, but they do not make it just as they please; they do not make it under self-selected circumstances, but under circumstances existing already, given and transmitted from the past."[10] Here we can see the importance of structure, but

Marx is still cognizant that humans retain the capacity to make their own history. The sociologist Dave Elder-Vass notes that there is much debate, amongst sociologists in particular, about how best to describe and address the interaction between structure and agency but says that we should focus our analysis on the overlapping and intersecting nature of these phenomena. Elder-Vass contends that, in and of itself, this debate really gets to the heart of some of the biggest questions we find ourselves exploring as social scientists.[11] Here, as an example, we return to the parents, carers, and communities who care and advocate for our neurodiverse and disabled siblings to illustrate the pressures structure imposes on individual agents to fulfil responsibilities. All the will in the world among a surplus of inequities like classism and racism does not guarantee an ordinary and dignified existence.

Our contribution to these debates around structure and agency engages intentionally with love, the emancipatory possibilities of the politics of neurodiversity, and the dismantling of neurotypical hegemony. Despite how things currently stand, the existing structures of society can be dismantled to better accommodate all neurominorities and majorities. This can be achieved by exposing and questioning the structures produced by neurotypical hegemony while at the same time working on processes of agential self-actualization, or people's ability to love themselves and those around them.

Through a discussion of insider-focused work on neurodiversity, and ADHD specifically, scholars such as Hanna Bertilsdottir Rosqvist and her colleagues are working through these tensions by asserting the possibilities of collective spirit while paying close attention to the varying needs of others.[12] Recognizing the indomitable impact of structure while also producing dialogues and practices of resistance is where we see a clear-cut connection between love, the neurodiversity paradigm, and disability justice. Love is one of many answers and we see a theory of love as a reclamation of scholarship that has always already been rooted in an empathetic ethics concerning the tension between structure and agency.

Coming back to our earlier point about the way that our perspectives on love are formed, it is clear to us that part of the tension between structure and agency informs the ways we have come to talk about and discuss the politics of neurodiversity. In this way we bring to this discussion our perspectives on love, which have been fundamentally tainted by people asserting their own agency to be (un)loving of neurodivergence and difference more broadly. By contrast, a lack of close attention to the pervasive and intense impact of structure on the most marginalized is another thing that requires attention. These realities make clear that it is too simple to claim that people can "choose" to dismantle neurotypical hegemony. But we can do our best to provide the tools for people to become increasingly aware of how ableism is normalized and we see this as rooted in conscious political education.

Whilst this fusion of a theory of love and political education is how we came to write this book, we must also acknowledge and reconcile with the fact that some people are fundamentally opposed to an ethics of love or an appreciation and acceptance of difference, simply because there is money to be made in creating a culture that abhors anything deemed to be 'different' or 'other.' This culture is the antithesis of love and it is, of course, fear. Fear of change or fear of anything unknown is how common sense and hegemony keeps themselves in check. Fundamentally, fear is what makes it impossible to question the existence of capitalism as the hegemonic social structure. This is why love can often feel like a utopian vision for society. Fear dampens our imagination, prevents us from dreaming and separates us from humanist endeavors; it stops us thinking of ourselves as a collective rather than as separate entities. But, as we write and acknowledge this reality, our optimism remains intact!

Introducing Love and Genuine Love

This book is the first project either of us have ever produced on the possibilities of love. To go back and forth between ideas around structure and personhood, and then to contemplate routinely what we mean by a praxis of love in relation to the politics of neurodiversity felt radical and challenging, but also very natural. Bringing some of the terms around notions of living and loving that we felt were most inspiring to us has now become incredibly important to the way we write and think as public sociologists. And with this, the journey we anticipate that you will embark on as you read this book is very much situated in the possibilities of love to guide us all in our quest for social justice for everyone. Of course, many—especially our critical academic friends—will read statements like this as an overindulgence in feelings and emotions when it comes to addressing systemic inequality. And, to some extent, we both understand and agree with the owners of these critical views. To assume that we can *love our way out* of the systemic inequality that plagues society on both local and global scales would be naïve. We do, however, want to distance ourselves from an analysis that situates perspectives on emancipation as either "wrong" or "right." Our emphasis on love throughout this book does not insist that love is the only way, but that it remains a necessary part of all conscience-driven social justice work. We are very much in the business of stressing its importance, as we highlight the failure to name love as an inherent part of how we both live and understand each other. In the politics of neurodiversity, and the multitude of ways it can help us imagine equity for everyone, we see frameworks of love as an integral point of analysis. A fundamental reason for this is that in many ways the framework of love is something that exists within our social relations already. A vision of the politics of neurodiversity and love is about recognizing a process, as well as a praxis, of naming. Put simply, love is something we learn, become, and later, know. Like the peripheral cultures that disabled people create in order to survive ableist society, love is omnipresent. Both disability and love exist, and both need radical attention if we are to truly support and advocate for everyone.

So before we get into how we are interpreting our theory of love and its relevance for the politics of neurodiversity, we will regularly remind our readers of the simple fact that neurodiverse people are part of society. In spite of our development of peripheral cultures and practices to survive neurotypical society, we are here and we are present. We deserve access to an ordinary life that is both dignified and loving. Part of our reasoning for making love such a central tenet of our analysis in this book is that it is the great unifier. It is what we all want—to belong, to have peace, and to be respected. Access to these things is mitigated by the structures of society such as race, class, and gender. Crucially, however, we are among those who believe that the treatment of disabled people in society is a very clear indication of the lack of a universal acceptance that we all deserve love.

A part of our framework of love also connects to one of the key threads of this book, which draws on different ways of producing hopeful anecdotes, perspectives, and imaginings for the future of society. We utilize bell hooks' notion of *genuine love* as providing the ongoing motivation to make neurodiverse lives more liveable (see chapter 3).[13] Genuine love is understood as a way of loving that many of us are already socialized to experience and strive for. Genuine love is seldom concerned with immediate gratification; it is built through time and commitment. This comes from the lessons in love we learn through relationships with friends and families. We lean on the merits of this love but draw on its complexities and uncertainties as a way to show how some of its dialects can also obscure emancipatory conversations about life. Put simply, it is not a given that we will experience genuine love in our families, in spite of society's continual emphasis that the site of unconditional love is within the biological family or in strong communal bonds. This is a reminder that love is work, and it is not a guarantee. It requires acknowledgement of social truths, such as the pervasive impacts of patriarchy and racism, whilst also doing the messy but integral work of recognizing how we ourselves are susceptible to producing both harm and lovelessness.

hooks reminds us that understanding genuine love is also an intentional practice that is deeply grounded in a politics of spiritual transformation rather than something that will save us on its own. Recognizing the merits of genuine love also allows us to make space for its limitations, which we find in the tension between an ongoing situating of self-actualization and a recognition of the structures that hinder this process. We use the term self-actualization here alongside the teachings of both Black feminist thought and humanist Marxism. It draws on a process of knowing ourselves in relation to the structures we find ourselves negotiating within our daily lives. It is about producing an ongoing relationship with ourselves grounded in recognition of our needs, values, and desires. Crucially, this is about connecting with a type of consciousness-raising which can be linked with, and of course mitigated by, structures of race, class, and gender, specifically. As Hill Collins has noted, when Black women specifically engage in the process of self-actualization, their perspectives offer other subordinate groups ways of knowing their social positions that can build a multitude of interlocking political transformations.[14] This is of course associated with our earlier discussions about the tensions between structure and agency—to what extent do societal structures hinder or provide space for an engagement with love? Self-actualization allows us to both produce and receive love, which takes into consideration that it is something that is demonstrated rather than a given. Self-actualization provides the space for us to see ourselves as producers of both harm and love while still being worthy of love. Put simply, it is not enough to say, "*we love,*" although there is resistance to this fact, tied to cultures that have asserted that love is about gestures rather than a way of being and relating to one another. Working through these processes of how to apply a framework of love, theoretically, is about *"effort, accountability, working your lives through and around each other. Active presence."* The connection between committing to processes of genuine love and self-actualization provides us with the groundings to begin to understand and see the value in one another's presence. This philosophy contends that the more we work on understanding ourselves in relation to structure, the more transformative a politics of knowing and loving can be for the rest of society.[15]

The Connection Between Love and Neurodiversity

Love is the praxis, the journey, and the ongoing challenge. The varying ways in which neurotypical hegemony penetrates every aspect of society make this path not only challenging, but near impossible for everyone. An intentional engagement with the theory and embodiment of love requires a complete reimagining of how we understand human life. Life is worthy of love, dignity, and freedom as a result of its occurrence; we need to remove the idea that to be worthy something needs to be "proven." Here, there is an obvious connection to be made between love and neurodivergence. The connection relates not only to silence but to assumptions about what both words mean in the everyday sense. As we outlined in chapter 1, we see representations of both neurodiversity and love as tending to individualize the meaning of both. Without a wider recognition of the structures that exist to generate these representations, we fail to truly take seriously what love and neurodiversity mean, in context and, crucially, in everyday life. This is where Black feminists and Marxists in particular warn of the perils of capitalism in its ongoing attack on our position in society. As value has become such an integral facet of human life, it makes sense that a lack of access to loving frameworks in society is tied to our proximity to productivity (see chapter 6). And productivity becomes aligned with both deservingness and respectability when it comes to our vision for love. We contend that one of the ongoing questions that civil society requires its members to ask is: "Is this person productive enough to receive love and acceptance?" Or, in the case of the politics of neurodiversity, "is this person's proximity to neurotypical ways of being and living close enough to a version of productivity that we value to be deserving of love?"

Neurodivergence and disability have been something for people to "put up with" rather than to love and respect. The Black feminist teachings of scholars such as bell hooks, who asserts that failure to discuss love is what makes lovelessness prevail, help us to understand our lived experience in relation to structure and agency. What makes this an intense and important issue in the case of neurodiversity is the lack of discussion of everyday practices for neurodivergent people as well as the lack of consideration of the importance of love in everyone's lives. Part of our work as critical scholars is about being clear that we are not above discussing the everyday—the parts of life that make it more liveable.[16] What we mean here is that aspects of living and feeling need to be considered in relation to how we live and understand each other. Failing to contextualize what we mean by love—in theory and in practice—creates a culture in which people assume that they are loving people, or that they always "know" how to be more loving. If we do not create the space to talk about the fluid yet intentional aspects of love, we continue to fail to fully understand one another. It is for this reason that we see an obvious connection between the politics of love and neurodiversity.

Part of emphasizing the nature of a society described through the cultures that neurotypical hegemony generates is also about re-capturing the disabled self, which is formed through the image of ableism. The effect of this on our disabled siblings has been addressed by leading disability scholars, who note that the emotional toll of oppression needs our ongoing attention if we are to truly address the essence of what ableism, in particular, does to the way people are viewed, cared for, and understood.[17] If we are constantly producing, across civil society, the idea that proximity to neurotypical functioning and the able body produces the most desirable citizen, we have to take seriously the ways in which this process becomes synonymous with lovelessness. We are constantly creating an image of love that is reduced to the idea that some people are *easier* to love than others. With notions of disability and neurodiversity associated with challenge, difficulty, and sometimes even stress for people who do not identify as disabled, and neuromajorities, we are normalizing lovelessness as tantamount to ordinary life while also showing the disabled community, specifically, that love is conditional.

This social reproduction also speaks to what Goodley understands as the critical turn in disability studies, in which deficit approaches and languages can be located in cultures that validate themselves through the ongoing creation of an Other in opposition to the able self.[18] Here, our commitment as disability scholars is to constantly turn the mirror back onto society—a society that tempers love and value with social structures that hinder the lives of all people. This lovelessness through cultures of ableism is evidently embedded in harms to the self through what Gorton says are the ongoing affect and emotion attached to the feelings created by the public sphere, which become lived and experienced in our bodies and minds.[19] Put simply, the mental and emotional toll of ableism needs more thorough attention (see chapter 3).

Through our analysis, we stress that our Black and neurodivergent subjectivity, as well as the teachings of Black feminism and Marxism, help to generate perspectives from which to address a multitude of societal inequalities. Our emphasis on subjectivity, capitalism, and how we relate to each other provides a unique vista for attending to inequality on a broader scale. Talking *with and about people* and centering the effect of social structures on how we relate to each other is where we see sites of love, hope, and solidarity. In this way, we take seriously the everyday aspects of love by naming exactly how we understand it in practice. The proliferation of notions of romantic love across civil society embeds myths concerning cultures of gestures and words. It is these more vacuous cultures of love that make lovelessness endure. We do not return to this point to set out the parameters of love, but rather to say that it needs to be expanded and understood as praxis, rather than just as feeling.

This issue around the discourse of love is integral to, and also mirrors, that of neurodiversity. We see this as the bridge between love and neurodiversity: to understand and recognize it, it has to be understood as descriptive, lived and intentional.

Love as the Praxis, Lovelessness as the Challenge

One of our main objectives in writing this book was to contribute to discussions about what it means to *live, think, and be* loving. We find genuine love in experiencing life in a way that allows us all to live in a dignified way and learn about who we are and how we would like to be in this society. Love is access to sufficient sanitation, housing, and space; it is access to community through friends and family; to work-life balance; to leisure, joy, and entertainment, but also space to feel emotions of frustration, sadness, and anger. To be loved and to feel loved is to exist in a world that won't dispose of us and accepts us in all our intricacies. In comparison, we understand lovelessness as the inevitable result of a culture that sustains itself by finding the value of human life at the junctures of ableism, racism, and capitalism. A loveless culture is the antithesis of care and restoration; it leaves no space for difference and stratifies livelihoods through race, class, gender, sexuality, and nation. We understand lovelessness as synonymous with the way society treats disabled and neurodivergent people. Crucially, the existence of both disability and neurodivergence are intersections at which these stratified livelihoods converge and are highlighted. Though the realities of this are clearly depressing, we see the direct correlation between ableism and lovelessness as providing generative routes into collective repair, renewal, and restoration in the name of equity and emancipation. Part of our process in this book involves paying specific attention to the structures, social processes, and institutions that rely on the engagement of everyone in society in cultures of lovelessness. Alongside this, we are clear that in our proposition to use a framework of love to better understand and accept neurodivergence, we are simply contributing to existing scholarship and activism that is committed to enacting and embodying theory and practice (praxis)—much of which already exists and has been imagined and enacted by our disability rights siblings—to produce loving cultures of difference.[20] We come to these discussions about how to define love, and how we can better embody and reflect it in our social relationships, from inside a society that routinely creates loveless environments. Clearly, this attempt to understand love while living amongst so much lovelessness is an imperfect process. We lean into these imperfections as part of a commitment to recognizing the humanity in coming to a loving praxis of analysis. In this way, it is only through our commitment to a detailed examination of how specific interpersonal and structural formations of lovelessness endure that we can really begin to see the routes to, and roots of neurotypical hegemony.

What do we mean, specifically, when we refer to lovelessness and loveless cultures? We frequently use the phrase "loveless cultures" to describe the primary consequence of neurotypical hegemony (or power). But in the context of laying out our framework of love, it is important to keep signalling back to the challenge at hand. We live in a society where human life is marketed in conjunction with productivity (see chapter 5), which in turn produces a culture in which value becomes a measure of who deserves love, in our sense of the word. In the context of the politics of neurodiversity and as we delve more deeply into our analysis of neurotypical hegemony, our reflections on the question of who is positioned as deserving of love are not reserved for the able-bodied or neurotypical majority. Essentially, what we see is a culture where access to resources (and cash) provides you with a more linear route, not only to *"come as you are,"* but also to be seen as worthy of love. We are not in the business of contributing to arguments that focus on a race to the bottom, but we are clear that whether you are disabled, neurodivergent, or able-bodied, the structures of society generate a hierarchy of people deserving of love. While this hierarchy is integral to the book and something we will repeatedly flag, we remain unconvinced that even those who experience relatively straightforward proximity to multiple streams of capital are themselves content. Of course, to have the resources to manage everyday life is an immense privilege, but our understanding of love is much more circular and collective. Put simply, when lovelessness exists, it finds ways to present even in the lives of those who apparently benefit from the way it is reproduced via capital. We only have to look at the number of people, globally, who are making the choice to take medication to help them feel more balanced and at ease with life. There is no judgement in this statement. It is more for us to begin to recognize that a fearful and traumatized society is one that is multiclassed, multiethnic and multigenerational. As we have already said, access to resources does make life more liveable but we continue to bear witness to the fact that those struggling with our loveless society come from all walks of life. None of us are free unless we are all free.

A Sociological Commitment to Self-Love and Self-Actualization

The central argument of the book insists that loving frameworks are vital if we are truly to work towards cultures resistant to neurotypical hegemony. When we began writing, it was clear to us that conversations about love were going to be integral to our broader arguments. Writing about love as we attempted to work out how to be loving beings ourselves was no easy feat. But as we drew on our lived experience as well as on historical and existing policy, and on structures that marginalize neurodivergence, we also wanted to stress that to love and be loved as neurodivergent people in this society is an ongoing challenge. In a world where physical and neurological difference seem so often to be regarded as abnormal, peculiar, and detrimental to the idea of a productive society (and workforce), self-love is a lifelong challenge. As we laid out in our introduction, neurotypical hegemony is understood to be of optimal value. That we have imagined and produced our worlds in this way is fundamentally linked to the challenge of self-love. What does it mean to receive daily reminders that your existence will merely be tolerated unless you can prove that your difference is something that can be converted into capital? The journey of self-love as disabled people in an ableist world is an enduring one, which can often feel like swimming against the tide of society. We are committed to this journey, however, to fight for more emancipatory futures for our neurotypical as well as our neurodivergent siblings. The practice of self-love is for everyone, even if at times we feel we are in the group that is climbing the hill furthest from the peak.

Our sociological training made our earlier conversations on the structural importance of self-love feel somewhat misplaced. But here we come back to the merits of collective scholarship and coming to our ideas together. It was only through our conversations about the politics of neurodiversity and love that we were able to lean into the fact that a commitment to self-love was a crucial part of how we could write a book about love with straight faces(!). As social scientists, we resist looking at individuals (and especially at ourselves), because our focus is so often on power and structure. We do understand that people have agency in shaping the structures of society, but this is often expressed as the starting point for consideration. Lived experience only tells us the first part of the story. It is not that we want to depart from our sociological training in this book, but we are arguing that in order to build loving frameworks to dismantle the structures that marginalize us, we must commit to self-actualization and self-love. Invariably, we return to our lived experience and personal relationships, or our (lack of) proximity to society's ways of marginalizing neurodiversity, and part of this commitment involves, additionally, an ongoing engagement with race, gender, and class. Our experiences of ableism differ, and our acknowledgements of this are stratified and understood within contexts of power and privilege. So as sociologists—yes, the rumors are true!—we nevertheless believe that an emancipatory framework can only be realized in its totality if we strive for an authentic engagement with the journey of self-actualization and self-love. We have to understand and love ourselves in order to show up better in society. To better equip the reader—and even if our own engagement with self-love needs a lot of work (it does)—we must still be clear about its importance, because loving frameworks are required for the dismantling of neurotypical hegemony. Self-love as praxis is a commitment to creating an internal space for loving others as well as ourselves, in a world fixated on lovelessness. Love in life and scholarship is a challenge, but we are committed to drawing on its revolutionary possibilities.

Writing with Black subjectivity and Black feminism

Now that we have outlined our theorical framework of love with the help of the teachings, cautions, and reflections of our fore parents, in this section we address how we wrote this book.

The framework of love forms the political and spiritual grounding of our reflections and provocations, and we accompany this with our subjective, theoretical, and methodological commitment to Black studies by way of Black feminism and Marxism. This is about practice, praxis, and intention and how we capture emancipatory dialects through the histories of Black people's collective and specific struggles and negotiations both locally and globally. Storytelling, autoethnography, and the situating of the self are processes of reclaiming, stating, and existing that Black scholars and creatives have specifically leaned into, to draw on the heterogeneity of life itself. How we wrote this book together very much followed the trajectory of our fore parents—exploring how we come to be part of social life by way of gendered racialization, further stratified by disability as well as self-actualization. We came to a conversation about Blackness and neurodivergence through our own personal relationships with these structures, to explore the struggle as a way of reaching hope and solidarity. This is where we see the work of bell hooks, again, as incredibly useful, not only for the methodological process but also for the visions we hope this book will inspire—it is all about self-love as a means of creating cultured and universal love. Generating compassion for ourselves by talking about our lives in civil society collectively provided us with the space to think critically about how we create dialogues and practices of empathy and understanding for people who have not walked the same paths as us. We have used bell hooks' notes on the value systems we create by living in service to others. Service to others by way of understanding difference which is beyond our own lived experience, strengthens our insight and compassion for others. All this being said, the ways in which ableism and the social reproduction of neurotypical hegemony impact our trajectories and writing as Black people are still things we return to throughout the book. This is about a process of reconciling the universal with the particular to begin to evoke what it means to write about society through our Black and neurodivergent subjectivities, while also looking at how our experiences can relate to, inform, and support others.

The Process

Before we get into the theoretical connection to practice and how we infused our process of analysis with Black feminist teaching, we want to name a few of the more personalized methodological processes we have used in writing this book. We were inspired by creative, spiritual and music-laden interventions when developing our method.

Recorded Conversations and Transcriptions

When we first started writing, we organized our ideas into themes that drew on our lived experiences of grappling with neurotypical hegemony. We thought about Blackness, gender, and family, but also about value and subjectivity. We thought about how and where we had grown up between the English Suburbs and London. We also thought about what we had witnessed in our jobs as sociologists. The core themes we decided on were education, mental health, capitalism, racism, and social and political dialogues (how people in general are spoken about in the media). For over a year we sat at a combination of kitchen tables, work desks, and coffee shop tables talking about what these core themes meant to us personally. We recorded twenty conversations on our smartphone software, which provided us with transcripts of our dialogues. In true neurodivergent processing and coordinating style, we repeated and returned to each topic over and over again. Each session would last between two and four hours and literally required us to talk, talk, and talk. Our analysis developed during our conversations with each other and really showed us the possibilities of intentionally making the process of "speaking" a formative and integral part of writing a book. As we both have backgrounds in broadcasting and podcasting, we were able to talk for long periods and draw on a variety of intersectional themes that correlated with the core theme we were focusing on during a session. In this way, and as can be seen through the ways in which this book has been put together, everything overlaps and everything is relatable. We found that speaking together in a disciplined, focused, and fluid way allowed us to show how issues are related to each other— like the question of how class sizes and environmental stimuli relate to mental health, or how "value" relates to the histories of Black resistance—issues that inspire every page of this book. Once we had finished recording these conversations, we spent a further four months organizing the core themes and sub-themes we had developed during this time. This process drew on our rich histories of building knowledge together and in community. Finding differences and commonalities through dialogue is very much where we see the tools for dismantling neurotypical hegemony. We also see how this process demonstrates the power of technological advances when it comes to thinking critically about how we imagine a better world. The fact that we could record our conversations and that they would automatically be transcribed ready for us to organize into book chapters will never not feel incredibly novel to us. Thank you in advance to the scholars and digital enthusiasts reading this and thinking: "wait till we tell you what else technology can do!?" The power of dialogue is something from which we drew strength and inspiration during the process of writing this book.

Emptying our Minds: Meditation, Prayer, and Karaoke

"You need to empty your mind, CJ"—Jason said to Chantelle during the many occasions we attempted to join-up so many of our thoughts and feelings about the topics in this book. While we have been clear about the possibilities of working in collaboration on a topic like neurodiversity, another key part of our process was leaning into solitude and thinking while being apart from each other. In particular, the power of prayer and meditation was a crucial part of how we came to arrive at our ideas and reflect on how we wanted to communicate to our readers. We remain resistant to the idolization of the lone scholar but would be doing a disservice to our prose and process by not mentioning that our ideas were also produced away from each other and away from the computer screen. Freeing our minds from thinking by using intentional practice with meditation was a crucial part of our praxis mainly because these matters are deeply personal. Rather than ignore and disassociate from the feelings that emerged when thinking about topics that caused us distress as both children and adults, we went into these feelings in meditation. We each looked at them to understand where they sat within our sense of self, and thus how we could move beyond the feelings to form a politics which communicates their impact on wider groups and society. For example, returning to childhood memories of both racism and ableism in both meditation and solitude allowed us to find the parts of us that were still pained by these experiences, seek to accept them, and later convert these feelings and experiences into communicating about political, social, and emotional education for others. Throughout his life, Fanon was acutely aware of the impact of subjugation on oppressed people, their identities and sense of self. He routinely wrote about the types of people and societies we were creating if we failed to look at the negative impact that hierarchies of humanity were having on the psyches of all people. Alongside this, Fanon was also clear that in order to claim one's life, humanity, and identity, positive affirmations of self-consciousness, awareness, and actualization were crucial for any kind of moves towards freedom and liberation, materially, socially, and spiritually.[21] We take these lessons from fore parents like Fanon, and in the process of writing this book recognized that a crucial requirement of thinking, writing, and imagining with heavy topics requires an *emptying of the mind*.

Now, returning to our more collective and music-laden approach to writing this book, we come to one of the more novel methods we used when it came to putting our ideas onto the page—karaoke. During the process of writing this book we spent many evenings in karaoke booths singing our hearts out to our favorite rock'n'roll, psychedelic, and consciousness-raising songs. While the politics expressed in the music and by our artists of choice did not always match up to the message of hope, love, and solidarity in this book—our singing duets ranged from REM to Oasis, Ocean Colour Scene, The Rolling Stones, Fleetwood Mac, Pulp, Blur, WHAM!, The Police, UB40, and Michael Jackson (to name just a few)—the repetition and routine of karaoke provided us with sensory relief and release which proved to be a crucial mechanism we could use during the more challenging moments in the writing process. Karaoke was a source of inspiration and the act of singing lyrics that draw on social commentaries proved to be an innovative way for us to retrieve our sociological imaginations when thinking about how we could create threads and narratives in this book that would bring as many people with us as possible.[22] Music is an art form that on many occasions has done the complicated work of changing hearts and minds, and it was the spiritual pull of the process of singing that not only guided us but at times also alleviated some of the pressures we felt when putting this together. As neurodivergent people, multisensory ways of communicating have enabled us to better understand intimate, social, and structural engagements *in and with society.*

Patricia Hill Collins and Afrocentric Feminist Epistemology

We end this chapter by introducing the ways in which we are applying theory and praxis throughout the book, with the help of Patricia Hill Collins' four dimensions of Afrocentric epistemology. In chapter 1 we spoke about the process of writing and thinking with and through friendship. While we understand that producing work with colleagues who are also friends is far from novel, we do see naming the "how" of how we have come to do this as particularly useful for beginning to show how neurodivergent sociology emerges. So much of what we wanted to talk about in this book has come from a combination of our lived experiences and careers in education. Like many neurodivergent scholars and writers, we found the beginning stages of getting our ideas onto paper as challenging as it was exciting. How we could make sense of something so deeply personal and political while keeping our academic and critical analysis at the heart of the story we were looking to tell. And as with so many of our conclusions throughout this book, the answer was talking, sharing knowledge, and communicating *in process.* The framework we found most useful for critically working and thinking together on this book came from Patricia Hill Collins' four dimensions of Afrocentric feminist epistemology.[23] We found this framework particularly helpful as it does the work of grappling with the tensions already mentioned above—the tensions between structure, agency, and love.

A. **Lived experience as a criterion of meaning:** We draw on our own and others' lived experiences throughout to demonstrate how the act of living becomes a route to knowing. But this knowing needs to be supplemented, supported, and understood alongside other ways of knowing to create more fertile ground for solidarity across difference.

B. **The use of dialogue to assess knowledge claims:** Conversation creates connection and courage. Being in dialogue with people and finding routes for understanding each other is crucial for all social justice work. It requires levels of humility that at times feel challenging, but the rewards are so often felt at moments where dialogue feels like the most challenging choice. Each of us came to writing this book with experience of many institutional and social situations where it has been assumed that we "do not know." While we recognize that this experience has been informed by the fact that we have grown up and lived as adults in a society that routinely positions Black people as intellectually inferior, we have both witnessed that "know-it-all-ism" is not a quality aligned with freedom and emancipation. We sit comfortably in the unknowing of social life, and the use of dialogue to grapple with our uncertainties about society has been central to every chapter of this book.

C. **The ethics of care:** Care has been an essential part of how we position love as integral to the politics of neurodiversity. Being intentional about care in our ethical approach has meant looking very carefully at how we use language and communicate our ideas about difference throughout this book. We are able-bodied academics based at elite universities and are producing knowledge about people with whom we are not in community and with whom we do not share lived experience of negotiating the tensions between structure and agency. Our ethics of care has thus been reliant on reflexivity and simply taking our time. At times, incorporating an ethics of care for everyone felt challenging. It troubled us to think critically about our ways of writing and thinking about people who are part of institutions that enact harm. We want to speak honestly about this in an effort to recognize just how difficult it is to *de-individualize* harm and inequity. It feels challenging to remove the idea that there are good and bad people. In the afterword, when we wrote about ESN schools, it felt difficult to not lean into naming and shaming the participants in such harms as if their behavior reflected defects of character. Care must be universal and it cannot be conditional. It needs to allow space for growth and setbacks. Care, like love, must always prevail in this work.

D. **The ethics of personal accountability:** As public sociologists we recognize our role as knowledge producers who have the capacity to generate positive impacts across society. We also recognize that our role can cause harm. We lean into the fact that our loving intentions may not always translate into work that builds solidarity. Sometimes what we say and what we research might cause mistrust, caution, and division. Here, we return to the tension between structure and agency to address the fact that we are part of structures that have a history of creating unsafe ideas and environments. Our personal accountability as the authors of this book involves recognizing that some will find what we say inspiring, while others might see it as missing the mark. Personal accountability for us is also about calling on others and writing about the human capacity to take responsibility for the choices we make in the society we find ourselves in. This is by no means to be interpreted as a call for a politics of blame-and-shame, but more a political and spiritual call to resistance through self-actualization. By recognizing what we as individuals put into society and our relationships, and the histories that inform these exchanges, we can find ways to end patterns of harm and achieve more loving ways of being. Personal accountability is about recognizing what we give and take from others, and how a relationship with ourselves needs to be built around truths about who we are and who we aspire to be. We recognize our flaws; we work on them in our daily practice and we love ourselves and others regardless. This is personal accountability through method and life. For a book about the politics of neurodiversity—life is method.

We know what you're thinking. That these first two chapters were pretty weighty for a book about love and hope! We have used this time with you to explore and make clear that loving praxis is the challenge for all social justice work. The tensions we see as crucial to this work and the forthcoming chapters needed to be explored in a way that took to task what sometimes feels like the near-impossibility of being able to evaluate structures and our experience of them. Agency, or an individual's capacity to make different choices is of course implicated by histories of racism, ableism, and capitalism. But we wanted to show how this process does not have to be an inevitability if we have a more thorough understanding of how structures come to be maintained. The issues we explore in the next chapters relate to why it is fundamental to make clear the ways in which neurotypical hegemony impede our ability to find solidarities with each other in our differing experiences of social life. Our ongoing contention is that neurotypical hegemony is the antithesis of love in that it makes human life and our ability to access an ordinary and dignified existence conditional on markers of value and success. We needed the space in this chapter to show you how our back and forth between theory and practice is personal, political, spiritual, and intentional. It has involved us making clear exactly what love *has* got to do with it, the process of locating our provocations musically throughout, and finally how Black feminist method and thought remains integral to our arguments.

3

I'll See You on the Dark Side of the Moon

MENTAL HEALTH AND ILLNESS AND THE CONSEQUENCES OF NEUROTYPICAL HEGEMONY

And if the cloudbursts thunder in your ear
You shout and no one seems to hear
And if the band you're in starts playing different tunes
I'll see you on the dark side of the moon

(PINK FLOYD, 1975)

RELEASED AS part of Pink Floyd's 1973 album, *Dark Side of the Moon,* the eerie and poignantly crafted lyrics of the song "Brain Damage" seamlessly introduce our reflections in this chapter on the connections between mental illness, neurodiversity, and neurotypical hegemony. It has been widely purported that the "insanity" themed lyrics of "Brain Damage" were written about the former frontman and co-founder of Pink Floyd—Roger Keith "Syd" Barrett. Known for his stream-of-consciousness-

fused-with-psychedelia writing style, Barrett struggled throughout his life with drug addiction, social withdrawal, and what
might now be considered to be prolonged incidents of psychosis.[1] Barrett had been experiencing acute stress, caused by a
combination of fame, drugs, and the continued demise in his
relationships with other members of Pink Floyd. The lyric "And
if the band you're in starts playing different tunes" is a reference
to Barrett's behavior near the end of his tenure with the band,
when there were said to have been several occasions where Barrett played a different song from the rest of the band during live
performances. "Brain Damage" provides a lyrical storytelling of
Barrett's increasing departure from reality, which eventually resulted in his removal from the band, precipitating a psychotic
breakdown. Barrett's exit from Pink Floyd was made official in
April 1968. However, earlier that year, in January, the band had
chosen not to collect him ahead of a gig they were playing at
University of Southampton, indicating that his departure from
the band was part of a longer and more drawn-out process.
There have been many biographies of Barrett and commentaries
on his mental idiosyncrasies, many of which conclude that his
symptoms were indicative of a "schizophrenic." "Brain Damage"
seems to illustrate that he suffered from a fusion of immense
creativity, mental instability, and social isolation while still living
within the parameters of what is considered "normality." Thus,
we read these lyrics and listened to this song with feelings of
sadness and relatability as we contemplated how our own experiences of neurodivergence only amplify our awareness that our
own proximity to the dark side of the moon is heightened by the
ongoing impact of neurotypical society. We would learn later in
the process of writing the book that psychologists in particular
have recently begun to question the label of schizophrenic that
was applied to Barrett and suggested that he may in fact have

been autistic.[2] In the light of these evolved understandings of Barrett's life and neurology, the lyric *"You shout and no one seems to hear"* becomes rather unnerving and begins to take on a different meaning, as we reflect on the neurotypical domination and hegemony in the lives of many people like Barrett, who came of age at a time when neurodivergence and mental ill health resulted in societal ostracism; people were institutionalized and removed from social life. Of course, looking at the lives of artists and other people like Barrett, who had access to capital, is somewhat limited as a representation of the classed and social marginalization of disability. But it still gives an important glimpse into the way someone's proximity to mental and psychological unravelling can be intensified by what is considered normal, valuable, and ordinary in society.

Barrett's relationships (or lack of) with others, and the inevitable harms his addictions caused to himself and others are clearly an important part of the story. But what can also be read from this vignette is how Barrett's inability to participate in and contribute to Pink Floyd in a way that was deemed socially acceptable illustrates another *"brick in the wall"* of society's long history of ostracizing neurodivergent and disabled people who are unable to fit into what we have called "civil" society.

A Focus on the Neurodivergent Individual

As we delve more deeply into the dark side of the moon, or what we describe as the more personal and individualized consequences of neurotypical hegemony, it will come as no surprise to many of our sociologist peers that this third chapter was one of the last we put together. It all comes back to those pesky provocations we shared about structure and agency in chapter 2. We remain drawn to the possibilities of looking at individual agency and the personal costs of structure as a stepping stone to a greater collectivizing of multiple social justice issues. But we would be doing a huge disservice to our multiethnic and multi-classed neurodiverse siblings if we did not address the fact that to move beyond how we feel or experience neurotypical hege-mony individually is a utopia and paradise which still seems something that can only be imagined at this stage in human his-tory. It is the political paradise that we might never be fully able to sit in comfortably because the mental implications of ableism routinely become such a huge part of our daily negotiations with society. We are human beings, and the matters we discuss throughout this book affect our sense of self, how we feel, and how we see ourselves and others. The constant evolution of rac-ism and ableism by way of capitalism is an endurance sprint for so many of us—the ongoing question is whether our minds are flexible enough to recognize its perils. To what extent are we able to keep a positive mindset as we grapple with the overlapping of so many intersectional inequities at once? How many times can we think and talk about inequity while things seem so desperate on both an individual and structural level for so many people? Because of this, we feel this chapter will be an important one for readers to return to as you make your way through the book. It is a reminder of the human cost of neurotypical hegemony; of how matters related to ableism, racism, and capitalism are public health issues first and foremost.[3] Moreover, they are issues that continue to have a demonstrable impact on the mental health and wellbeing of neurodivergent people and their families. In line with our understanding of the politics of neurodiversity throughout, we recognize this chapter's intervention as one that signifies how these issues impact everyone in society and need a public response. But the crux of the chapter is located in the consequences of having to consistently conceal the existence of one's neurodivergence over time. These consequences produce cultures in which our neurodiverse siblings come closer to both spiritual and actual death.

Turning to the more individualized consequences of ableism produces a more intimate and critical conceptualization of neurotypical hegemony in practice. We lean on our personal reflections on masking (autism) and adaptation (ADHD) as Black neurodivergent people. In this way, the chapter pays close attention to the simultaneity of neurodivergence and the depletion of mental and emotional wellbeing.

Love and hope are positioned as both radical and necessary frameworks for addressing these matters, as the consequences of ableism can prevent neurodiverse populations from living harmoniously alongside the neurotypical majority, both as children and adults. Judith Butler's concept of *liveability* is presented as a symptom of neurotypical hegemony, whereby society's failure to critically engage with (mythical) universalist social reproductions of the human and its neurological functioning coincides with the ever-present possibility of *making unliveable lives*.

As we pointed out in chapter 1, there is an increasing volume of critical scholarship and resources that clearly describe how neurodivergent traits manifest themselves in social life—our job is not necessarily to contribute to these developments in disability work activism. However, as the authors of a book on love, neurodiversity, hope, and disability we feel we would be doing a disservice to our community if we did not spend time discussing and exploring the very real ways in which our neurodivergence interacts with mental health. Although we understand, and are very much writing against, the trend towards neoliberal approaches to neurodivergence,[4] we feel that if we are to humanize our struggle it is important to make clear the links between neurodiversity, mental health, and mental illness.

The issues we discuss in this chapter are multiethnic and multiclassed. They are issues that we all need to make an effort to understand. Fundamentally, concealing our neurodivergent identities can make us unwell. This reality can be applied to all forms of social identification such as gender, sexuality, religion, and ethnicity.

Critical Disability Studies: Language and Mental Illness

We feel incredibly privileged to be primarily based in the discipline of sociology, as the subject-matter encompasses a variety of subjects, which we feel gives us permission to engage with feelings and emotions, which might otherwise be seen as overly "subjective." Here, we intentionally note social phenomena that describe the tension between structure and agency; the tensions between what we experience as a result of history and biography and how this makes us feel, act, and behave as people in today's society. Put simply, we are Black and neurodivergent people with ancestry that cuts across histories of resistance, oppression, and ordinariness.[5] We are complex, heterogenous, and human.[6] This history informs how we see ourselves, and the way it is communicated and understood in civil society becomes crucial to how we find and build solidarities across difference. When it comes to mental health and illness, it is essential to write about its connection to neurodiversity in the language we use—how it makes us and others feel, and what it can provide for those of us seeking to claim self-actualization and inclusion in civil society. For this reason, language is important. We return to our sociological training to look at the way language becomes an important component of the intersections between mental health, mental illness, and neurodiversity because it allows us to pivot and lean on the revolutionary practices and lessons of critical disability studies.[7] Critical disability studies, by and large, encourages us to look at the experiences of disabled people through their engagements with the social and political structures that surround us. Ableism is constructed and consented to in our intimate, personal, and professional lives simply because we are required to engage with these parts of civil society if we are even to begin to grasp ordinary status. Critical disability studies wants us to challenge the pathologizing, pitying, and victimization of disabled people, and instead of looking at how we can change or correct ourselves we should look more at the failures of institutions, and the civil society around us. Aubrecht has noted that this turn in how we reconcile with disability, language, and movement in a society where ableist thinking is embedded demonstrates that this kind of critical approach to difference should now be understood as an essential form of political education.[8] When we begin to grapple with how this all relates to neurodiversity, we stress that proximity to mental health and illness language becomes an essential part of our stories since neurotypical society so often takes us away from presenting as, and being, ourselves.

When it came to the use of language in this chapter, we decided to use mental health and mental illness interchangeably. We see these terms as providing ways of knowing oneself and others, as deeply connected, and very much demonstrative of how life for many people is premised on the ability to get through the day, having to survive the social and material consequences of feeling out of alignment with oneself and others. We use "health" because if this is negatively impacted it has the capacity to impede our ability to participate in civil society in a dignified way. Poor health impacts our presents and futures; it can be short term, long term, or lifelong. Health is wealth. Similarly, we recognize illness as a crucial label for our contentions because it is historically loaded with the stigma and lived realities of living on the margins of society.[9] Our use of illness is a political reclamation of a word that has been used to cause harm to our neurodiverse and mentally ill siblings for generations. Reclaiming it as a way to speak back to and expose this history and present-day experience is part of our commitment to loving political education. Here, we are inspired by the provocations of people such as Aubrecht and Titchkosky, who have contested the use of "People First Language" when talking about disability and mental illness.[10] They note that language such as a "person with a disability, or person with mental illness" fails to systematically improve our collective understandings of what it means to embody disability and mental illness amongst ableist cultures. Aubrecht stresses that emphasizing "with"—as in a person *with* mental illness—is a way of seeing and labelling disability and mental illness as an "add on." It creates a vernacular where it is assumed that we can distance ourselves from the embodiment of disability and mental health and illness.[11] Here, we turn back to Patricia Hill Collins and the power of lived experience in methods as a tool for speaking back to social structures and ideas that affect how we understand ourselves and others in society. Language is important, and efforts made to incorporate "people first" language into the discussion of disability and mental health and illness clearly aim to adhere to the critical disabilities studies endeavor to shine a light on external structures, values, beliefs, and institutions, while simultaneously accessing the lives of disabled people and communities. But when it comes to matters of the mind, distancing oneself from the bodily reality of disability through the use of language may not always provide us with the freedoms produced by the rejection of other categorizing labels. Put simply, for some of us, going more deeply into the emotional, visceral, and multisensory experience that neurodivergence and mental health and illness can produce could be an essential part of how we become more confident and at peace with the complex process of self-actualization.

Some Terminology:
Masking and Emotional Dysregulation

In this section, we introduce the concepts of autistic masking and ADHD emotional dysregulation (ED) as examples of the mental and psychological consequences of adapting to neurotypical hegemony. We draw on autism and ADHD as reminders to readers of our lived experiences of both, as well as of our commitment to drawing on the social model of disability—our emphasis is always on the way society is organized, rather than on a person's perceived or labelled 'impairment' or difference. These are terms largely agreed upon within the neurodiversity movement as some of the ways that neurodivergent people conform or react to the valued and accepted ways of interacting with the social world. They are also social responses to neurotypical society, of which we have embodied and lived experience. We prioritize these examples in resistance to any kind of hierarchy of oppression caused by neurotypical hegemony, to recognize just how many different and often hidden ways neurodivergent people manage cultures of ableism. At the same time, in the spirit of accountability it is also important to note that while the links between masking, ED, and mental illness among neurodivergent people are clear to us, there are other social responses to ableism of which we have limited understanding. Further, there is a vast range of physical and neurological disabilities and their subsequent effects on mental and emotional wellbeing that will be missing from this chapter.

The simplest way to describe *masking* is as the act of hiding autism. Masking is the unconscious and subconscious suppression of one's own natural autistic responses in social interactions, sensory environments, cognition and behavior. In addition to this, "camouflaging" by presenting outwardly as "non autistic" is said to happen in tandem with masking.[12] It is all about the concealment of both self and identity and has now been shown to be linked to stress, mental illness, and suicidality.[13] Crucially, this process is about presenting outwardly in inauthentic ways in an effort to be valued and accepted as a member of civil society. Some examples of masking include learning and then subsequently copying neurotypical conversation patterns such as small-talk or stopping oneself from engaging in self-soothing behaviors that others find peculiar like waving your arms, rocking back and forth, wanting to eat the same food every day or simply wanting to listen to the same song on repeat.

Though emotional dysregulation is not exclusive to the ADHD community, it can be a prevalent feature of ADHD, impeding an individual's capacity to "select, attend to, and appraise emotionally arousing stimuli."[14] The definition we felt most aptly described ED was that of Shaw et al:

> Emotional expressions and experiences that are excessive in relation to social norms and are context inappropriate; 2) rapid, poorly controlled shifts in emotion (lability); and 3) the anomalous allocation of attention to emotional stimuli. Here, we focus on the clinical expression of emotion dysregulation as irritability, which is often linked with reactive aggression and temper outburst.[15]

We chose to couple autistic masking with ED in this way as we see these responses to social situations as demonstrating what is at stake in a society so little focused on how it could be more adaptable and inclusive of neurodiversity. While autistic masking for some creates social situations where someone is constantly seeking to find ways to hide their self and identity, ED can be understood simply as the condition of being over-stimulated by the past, present, and future of oneself and one's place in society. For some, ED can be the consequence of being unable to keep up with what neurotypical hegemony cultures deem acceptable. It encompasses a spectrum of responses which could result in more external outbursts, like shouting at others. Alternatively, it could be experienced as closing in on oneself, producing feelings of shame, inadequacy, and hopelessness. Pollak et al. have suggested that ADHD can manifest in some people "as a vulnerability factor for poor adaptation to life transitions and stressors."[16] The social and emotional effects of constantly failing to achieve what are considered to be reasonable, valuable, and acceptable ways of getting through life constitute the tension that ED creates.

Later in this chapter we turn back to masking and ED to highlight the connection between suicide and neurodiversity. We do this to illustrate some of the ways that adapting or reacting to neurotypical hegemony become completely unmanageable. While we look at how the individual or "agent" responds to normalized structures, cultures, and values, we see this as part of building our human stories concerning what is at stake when the human cost of ableism is hidden.

Naming our Resistance and Reluctance

While we come to the exploration of neurodiversity as Black neurodivergent people who see things through our sociological imaginations (our personal biographies and how they relate to the society we find ourselves in), we have been wary of drawing

on the known ways neurodivergent people cope with neurotypical hegemony and the mental and psychological harms they
cause. There are two key reasons for this reluctance, which
clearly demonstrate just how normal it has become to consent
to these sorts of harms in civil society. First, it can be emotionally challenging to talk about how we make sense of and then
live in cultures that marginalize our ways of being. These are
topics we spend our careers talking about—how we find ways
to mask and adapt in environments built to exclude us. We have
each made choices which mean that large parts of our lives in-
volve looking intimately at race and disability. We spend a lot
of time in professional spaces talking about these matters while
there continues to be very little change in how society values or
understands our communities. The result is that talking through
these mental and emotional harms can sometimes make us feel
we are attempting to fill an empty space. Secondly, as sociologists we often see any kind of overemphasis on individuality as
distracting from the structures that provide the groundings
(and the institutions) of the harms to the self we explore. In
chapter 2, we grappled with this tension between structure and
agency, but we still find ourselves returning to the fact that discussing the ways we cope—as individuals—with inequities of
race and disability has seldom made a local and global material
difference to the lives of the most vulnerable neurodivergent
and disabled people.

Over time, we started to understand that our reluctance to
write this chapter was a clear example of how neurotypical hegemony has affected our identities and sense of ourselves in ways
that have remained hidden even to two people working together
on a book that attempts to expose its harms. Fundamentally,
when we began to think critically about mental health and mental
illness amongst neurodiverse people our emotions immediately

became heightened. By intentionally seeking to unmask and resist adapting, simply by naming the health and mortality implications of neurotypical hegemony, we entered a position of vulnerability which for many neurodivergent and disabled people has not been met with love, care, and universal acceptance. So yes, we can sit and write about all the different ways in which a focus on individual harm can distract from the social reproduction of inequity, but by avoiding the emotions, feelings, and consequences for individuals we can also do the work of hiding the human stories of neurotypical hegemony. This in turn can distract from the ways that we can relate to and find solace, peace, and empathy in the lived experiences of others.

Sustained Damage

The damage we sustain in neurotypical hegemony involves emotional, spiritual, and social sacrifice; these are the concessions we make in our sense of ourselves. This damage resembles a cyst composed of cells that multiply many times over. Left undrained, the cyst causes a huge infection and damage for which there is no remedy. Every time we experience ableism it produces such unremitting damage. Our experience, and that of many neurodivergent people, has often involved suppressing natural behaviors, which requires a straddling of multiple personalities and continual code-switching in an attempt to conform to social norms. The enforcement of "typical behaviors" requires us to redefine what these behaviors are. Our society forces individuals to mask, with the punitive consequence of exposing those that do not. There is a tax to pay for such assimilation: increased anxiety, depression, and ultimately physical and metaphysical burnout. The tax is a heavy one for the neurodivergent individual attempting to establish a foothold in the exclusionary structures discussed throughout the book, ultimately compromising the sense of belonging we all yearn for. Mental health also becomes compromised through the stratification of identity and the enforced expectation that neurodivergent people must adopt ways of thinking that are binary, methodical, and normative. For example, if we fix our gaze on educational institutions—in this case in the UK context—the way we encourage our young people to learn and socialize is limited in terms of literacy about health and wellbeing. At the moment we continue to see this kind of emphasis on childhood development as an 'add-on' to core curriculum, rather than embedded in all learning. For the neurodivergent young person this is of course intensified by a lack of appreciation of how the norms of society, and even the little we do learn about health and wellbeing, are stratified by neurotypicality. This only becomes more acute as we move into adulthood, and many take their place within the labor market. The confrontational aspect of ableism somewhat resembles a situation in which the oppressed must continually face the source of their own oppression, something that can transpire daily for neurodivergent people. Our own traversing of this turbulent, thorny terrain has been difficult; citing discriminatory or exclusionary episodes is often (disappointingly) normalized. In some cases it is expected. The merging of these episodes creates a blurring of lines that can sometimes compromise our ability to challenge and question the reasons why neurotypical hegemony (for the most part) remains uninterrupted in our society. In some of the more painful examples of these episodes, we find ourselves confused and disorientated by the extent to which mental health is affected by the proximity between love and neurotypicality. Here, we are referring to the fact that even our friends and family are sometimes at risk of enacting the neurotypical hegemony that permeates mental health and wellbeing. And because of the intimacy involved in the production and normalization of neurotypical hegemony, our efforts to form loving cultures must take seriously the tensions between structure and agency. Here, we are referring to the fact that even those we are most closely bonded to become susceptible to reproducing these cultures, which takes a mental and physical toll. We emphasize this factor throughout the book to remind readers that it is useless to form resistance to neurotypical hegemony if we become wedded to the idea that its existence is in the hands of individuals. When we know there is evidence of genuine love between family and community but still see a simultaneity between neurotypical hegemony, normality, and value, then we know that our efforts would be wasted on simply blaming individual people.

Above, we have stressed our points about mental well-being in order to set up the theories we believe encapsulate what is at stake when our culture continues to neglect the ongoing consequences of neurotypical hegemony for both the self and society.

The Unliveable, Suicide, and Subjectivity

We turn now to how the tensions between neurotypical hegemony, structure and agency can create "unliveable lives," which can lead to depleted mental health for neurodiverse people. The unliveable is the most extreme point of human suffering and injustice. But what is it exactly? How do we define "unliveable"? And what can we do to prevent and repair it? These are the intriguing questions discussed by Judith Butler and Frédéric Worms in a captivating dialogue situated at the crossroads of contemporary life and politics. Butler criticizes the norms that make life precarious and unliveable (let's say anything from food and housing insecurity to domestic violence, as well as

genocide, war, and forced migration as examples), while Frédéric Worms appeals to "critical vitalism" as a way of allowing
the hardship of the unliveable to reveal what is vital for us—
suggesting that it is only through hardship that we are able to
see what is vital and necessity for us to live. We were drawn to the
concept of the unliveable as we began to think more deeply
about the connections between mental illness, neurodiversity,
and neurotypical hegemony because although it felt like a subjective term, it seemed to describe very well how the construction
of life itself can simply chip away at you. Life can feel unliveable
because of a lack of access to vital resources like food and shelter; but also due to the perils of consistently presenting oneself
through a mask. Being able to live authentically in one's skin but
also being able to clean and feed ourselves feels far from being
relatable in many ways. But when we look directly at the long-
term impact of neurodivergent coping mechanisms, we can see
just how intrinsic the marginalization of neurodivergence becomes to unliveable lives.

Suicide

Returning to the sustained damage cause by masking in autism,
we know that clinical levels of depression, anxiety, and suicide are
high amongst autistic people.[17] In Denmark, in their research on
suicide and masking, Kairi Kõlves, Cecilie Fitzgerald, and Merete
Nordentoft sought to answer the question: *Do people with autism
spectrum disorder suffer higher rates of attempted and actual suicide
compared with those without autism spectrum disorder?* They produced a nationwide retrospective study that included 6,559,266
people aged ten years or older living in Denmark between 1995
and 2016 and found that "individuals with a diagnosed autism
spectrum disorder had more than 3-fold higher rates of suicide

attempts and suicide compared with all other persons after adjusting for sex, age, and time period."[18] On a more international scale, in 2021, a conference report by the *Australasian Society for Autism Research* claims that:

> suicide attempts and deaths in autistic people . . . [are] three-to almost nine-fold greater than that seen in non-autistic people. With up to 24,535 suicide deaths in 2019, autistic people comprise up to 3.2% of suicide deaths globally.[19]

Turning to ADHD and the risk of suicide, there are strong links between research produced internationally that shows the connection between children and adolescents, and suicidal behaviors.[20] Other research is now seeking to show how these childhood suicide ideations follow people into adulthood. Hinshaw (2012) observed how higher rates of suicidal behavior amongst young women were connected to childhood histories of ADHD.[21] In autumn 2022, with research increasingly showing the connections between suicidal thoughts, suicide attempts, and death by suicide, ADHD UK announced a new research partnership with the University of Glasgow to explore the relationship between ADHD and suicide risk.[22]

These studies of autism and ADHD offer some of the more contemporary research on suicide and neurodiversity and show that society creates conditions that can produce feelings and emotions that result in fatal consequences for the neurodivergent individual. These outcomes are tied to mental health, mental illness, and the feeling that life is unliveable. We want to emphasize that these risks are both a symptom and consequence of neurotypical hegemony. In this way, the balancing act between neurodiversity and societal survival in a neurotypical world is often overwhelming, overstimulating, and disorientating. Difficulties may be suppressed, causing an enforced and often delayed trauma, which compounds the continuing feelings of isolation and exclusion. The reductionist approach generally applied to people in the neurodivergent community is one that sees them as intellectually inferior; it is underpinned by a narrative that aligns neurodiversity with a predisposition to compromised mental health. But as we contend throughout the book, this is an issue for all people. We continue to produce an inflexible society, and its customary and exclusionary nature affects both neurotypical and neurodivergent people.

Readers familiar with the work of Émile Durkheim will notice the influence of *Suicide* on how we have arrived at our reflections here.[23] In 1897, Durkheim published a groundbreaking sociological study of suicide, concluding that it had causes that were primarily social, rather than being the result of an individual's character or temperament. Among other things, he focused on the difference in suicide rates between Catholics and Protestants, concluding that Catholics had lower rates of suicide as a result of more socially cohesive communities and control (basically more social contact and cultural rules about remaining connected to people) in comparison to Protestants. While there have been many critiques of Durkheim's scholarship, many of which are worthy of further study, several of his findings are particularly useful in relation to suicide, unliveable lives, and the politics of neurodiversity under conditions of neurotypical hegemony.[24] One of his most distinctive findings concerned social integration, where the more someone is tangibly connected to a society (and its cultures), the more likely they are to feel a general sense of belonging and the less likely they are to commit suicide. Durkheim divided suicides into four categories:

i. Anomic: A sense of disconnection from society and a feeling of not belonging resulting from weakened social cohesion. This can occur during times of social and economic struggle that have a demonstrable impact on everyday life

ii. Altruistic: Suicide in the name of a social cause or social movement and the product of the excessive regulation of the individual

iii. Egoistic: Feeling completely detached from society due to the loss of family and community. A lack of contact with ordinary aspects of society such as education, work, and family

iv. Fatalistic: Occurs during more extreme scenarios where there might be institutional involvement that regulates movement; usually an oppressive condition where suicide feels like the only viable option.

We decided to loosely outline Durkheim's four types of suicide in this context—as part of a discussion of the impact of a dominant neurotypical hegemony on the neurodivergent sense of self and the cultures we navigate in society—as we felt it was useful to consider his observations against the backdrop of the arguments in the book. Crucially, what Durkheim showed is that feelings about self and self-worth (and whether a person believes they deserve to live) are connected to how we feel about the society we live in. Aside from altruistic suicide, what connects these descriptions are feelings of detachment, disconnection, and incidents of societal rejection (both perceived and actual). As we returned to Durkheim's analysis when writing this book, a sense of sadness and frustration often entered our conversations about neurotypical hegemony. It makes sense to us that many neurodivergent people see the only way towards freedom as ending their unliveable lives via suicide. Each of us is continually confronted with our experiences of navigating our psychological wellbeing, which have often been a result of having to oscillate continually between managing and suppressing our neurodivergent behaviors and ways of being in order to accommodate others, especially those who are frustrated with members of the neurodivergent community for their "inability" to assimilate. The short-term impact on self-esteem and confidence of masking, managing, and suppressing ourselves is palpable, but the long-term effects too often compromise psychological and mental wellness.

Mental Illness, Suicide, and Subjectivity

Chantelle: In February 2008, at the age of sixteen, I spent a forty-eight-hour period trying to take my own life, and as a result agreed to be voluntarily sectioned in a youth mental health facility. Although after a few weeks I managed to convince the psychologists that I could leave the facility, at no point during the psychiatric assessments I received either during or after being sectioned was there ever a suggestion that I might be neurodivergent. The events leading up to this suicide attempt primarily involved my own efforts to negotiate my lack of understanding of how to participate in social life with healthy boundaries, being confused by schoolwork, growing up with an incredibly isolated home life, and having very few family members and friends who shared my Black African heritage. Of course, at this point I was a teenager, a time of life that is challenging regardless of neurology. We know that an increasing number of young people are taking their own lives or self-harming.[25] I draw on my own lived experience of a suicide attempt not to exceptionalize my own plight, but rather to begin to illustrate how the pressures of neurotypical hegemony affect a subsection of people who see suicide as the only reasonable option. The reality of neurotypical hegemony is that it is only now, in my thirties, that I am really beginning to understand why life became so unliveable. Black and minority ethnic and working-class people who also happen to be neurodivergent are required to adapt to social life and hide in a way that not only feels unnatural to us, but that has been proven to affect our mental health and sense of self in the long term. In my case, and for many Black and neurodivergent people, this dysphoria merges with a combination of various structural insecurities that intensify feelings of stress, anxiety, and depression to levels that become not only unsustainable but deeply unliveable. There is a surplus of evidence that draws on the psychological and chemical imbalances caused by the process of presenting—outwardly—to the neuromajority, as non-neurodivergent. On top of this, we know that the distinct lack of research on race, gender, and neurodivergence has become untenable. This lack of knowledge continues to produce a culture where constant negotiation, masking, and adapting to neurotypical hegemony are the only ways to access (what is deemed to be) a valuable and ordinary existence.

Liveability

Returning to the unliveable, and the ideas of Butler and Worms, we reflect on the question of which people are provided with the time, or take the space to access, *liveability*, outside of struggle? Who is able to access a more linear experience of living with ordinariness and dignity? As sociologists, we are very much inspired by ideas of a *socially constructed* world in which everything from the ways our families are formed to education and the workplace, is a part of civil society that has been intentionally designed in line with certain beliefs and values.[26] Though these constructions are fluid, changeable, and clearly often in contention (see for example the arguments in this book!), we also see the possibilities in our ways of resisting norms as highlighting more concrete routes into what liveability looks like for all people. Perhaps, without the struggle, we are unable to locate what it truly means to know what we need for ourselves to access an ordinary and dignified existence. And maybe it is only through trying to live authentically that we can see what liveability means to us. We lean on these provocations and reasonings about living as we seek to imagine what it might mean to provide loving and caring environments for as many people as possible. Right now, the lives and liveability of people more able to access neurotypical ways of being are prioritized but even this does not guarantee their mental and emotional wellbeing. In 2019, according to the World Health Organization (WHO), and without controlling for neurodivergence, suicide was the cause of more than 700,000 deaths worldwide (representing about one point three percent of all deaths globally).[27] In 2016, suicide was among the top ten causes of death in Eastern Europe, Central Europe, Western Europe, Central Asia, Australasia, Southern Latin America, and high-income areas of North America.[28] Inserting the politics of neurodiversity into our comprehension of living provides multiple routes to understanding differences among people and recognition that the unliveable is largely influenced by the social structures we have dedicated much of this book to outlining. These are structures that impact the mental and emotional wellbeing of both neurominorities and neuromajorities.

Diagnosis, Parents, Carers

We can see the gap between the unliveable and liveability in the neurodiversity movement when we look at the diagnosis of neurodivergence, and at the parents, carers and communities of people who support our neurodivergent siblings to navigate neurotypical hegemony. At the time of writing, in 2024, we know that issues related to both diagnosis and tangible support for parents and carers remain a pertinent, and ultimately classed, issue for our movement (see chapter 5). Also, as Black people who were arguably diagnosed "too early" (Jason, at three years old) and "too late" (Chantelle, at twenty-four) we see the politics of diagnosis as a murky area—and one that is personally quite challenging to adjudicate during this phase of our lives and this stage of the neurodiversity movement. As we expressed earlier in the book, our intervention seeks to look at the sociology of neurodiversity and disability, rather than the psychology. This means that the tensions around the practical application of diagnosis are not part of our arguments for now.[29]

What we can see that is relevant for the arguments in this chapter is how both early and late diagnoses of neurodivergence reveal intersectional inequity that our research communities largely still fail to recognize and represent. In a 2016 study of ADHD diagnosis by Coker et al., a population-based, multisite sample of 4297 schoolchildren revealed racial and ethnic disparities in the diagnosis and treatment of ADHD among African-American and Latino children.[30] Black girls, women, and other genders are not receiving adequate support when it comes to diagnosis.[31] The Black and queer mental health advocate, writer, artist, and coach Nia Patterson critically discussed their lived experience of navigating the diagnosis process as one that is specifically exclusionary for Black trans people, concluding that, "An official diagnosis is just one piece of that. Advocating for yourself is just as important, if not more so."[32]

The racialized elements of diagnosis are clear and must also be understood alongside issues of class. Here in Britain, support for diagnosis, special needs education, and disability support more broadly is at breaking point.[33] We take this turn to the operation of race and class during diagnosis to help highlight not just the lives of the neurodivergent individual, but also their parents, carers, and supporters, whose advocacy inspires every page of this book; seldom do we make space for how neurotypical hegemony seeps into mental and emotional wellbeing. First the battle for diagnosis or recognition that a child needs greater support, then the battle to access resources for an ordinary and dignified life. Liveability and the ability to "live," for parents and carers of disabled children and adults in a society where neurotypical hegemony is so dominant, clearly has an impact on mental, emotional, and physical wellbeing.

In July 2023, we travelled to Rockaway in Queens (New York, USA) where Jason was giving a keynote speech at the Perfect Piece of the Puzzle Inc event, *YOU DESERVE . . . BRUNCH.* Perfect Piece of the Puzzle is a non-profit organization founded by Trishia Bermudez, who at sixteen weeks pregnant found out her unborn son had a chromosome deletion.[34] Bermudez used her lived experience of navigating the care of her son, who has multiple medical issues and special needs, as a route into the creation of an organization dedicated to supporting families of all ages to access care and resources in their local area. As Jason gave his speech at their annual brunch, which focused on "reminding caregivers that they are loved, thought of, cared for, and most importantly remembered for all that they do," we were humbled and inspired by this kind of radical recognition of love and care. The space was filled with honest conversations not just about the isolation experienced by families and communities—the result of caring in an ableist society—but also about the inevitable toll it takes on their mental and emotional wellbeing. This intergenerational space was one that highlighted the way that managing and negotiating neurotypical hegemony is a lifelong endeavor; these human stories of representation are necessary in order to truly begin to grasp the mental toll it can take on all those affected. We use our observations from the Perfect Piece of the Puzzle to emphasize our belief that liveability is where we can live to explain and tell our stories of struggle, hope, and ordinariness in community. This is an essential part of being human, and we see that ableism in particular limits the spaces in which we are able to do this. We also think the work of Jim Sinclair is particularly useful here, for loving reflections on grief, parenting, and autism.[35] Love, care, and support make human life liveable; that is, they make life "more than just living." Liveability in this way is about which people are given the space to share their stories of how they come to understand what is vital for them to feel belonging and cohesion in society. For the neurodiversity movement, the connections between liveability and the mental health and wellbeing of those who advocate for us is an essential part of how we imagine more equitable futures for us all.

Concluding Remarks

Throughout this chapter we have focused on the consequences of neurotypical hegemony on mental health and well-being. Our contentions have been focused on the question of which people are given the space to come as they are, and which must alter their sense of self to fit into (what has been deemed) a worthy, ordinary, and civil existence? In chapters 5 and 6 we take a deeper dive into race, class, capitalism, and value to demonstrate just how important it is to recognize the way these social and political processes become essential to the dismantling of neurotypical hegemony. Being on the dark side of the moon or experiencing mental illness is not limited to neurodiverse people and is a symptom of the way we live and relate to each other in modern society. The underlying principle of this chapter, which unites all people and social justice endeavors, is that there will always be those who are mentally unwell, which means that the creation of more loving, understanding, and accountable cultures of mental and neurological difference is crucial for all of us.

4

The Great Beyond

WHY THE (GLOBAL) INSTITUTION OF EDUCATION (STILL) MATTERS

I'm pushing an elephant up the stairs
I'm tossing out punchlines
That were never there
Over my shoulder a piano falls
Crashing to the ground

(REM, 1999)

WIDELY REGARDED as one of rock's first alternative bands, REM represents something entirely unique in the American and global music landscape. Bewitching with their semi-folk-rock ballads and melodic commentaries, they remain one of music's favorite outliers despite disbanding in 2011. The quote with which the chapter begins symbolizes the disorientating nature of what we later conceptualize as the "institution of education," which oscillates continually between assimilation and exclusion and can make you feel like you're either "in" or you're "out." Failure to fit into one of these camps can push some into apathy and self-loathing; in some cases it can result in alienation from learning. The people who understand the more detrimental effects of these challenges are those held back on the fringes and periphery of society. The possibilities and limitations of education for all of us can often expose some of the clearest dividing lines across society. While these dividing lines are evident both historically and in the present day, we find hope in the wisdoms of critical pedagogical thinkers like Paulo Freire, who reminds us of the liberatory possibilities of education grounded in cultural respect, humility, and understanding between the student and the educator, regardless of cultural difference.[1]

In this chapter, we take a voyage into *The Great Beyond* of the institution of education by looking at exactly what it is we promise people in society, as well as that which we collectively create and to which we consent. Here, we note that "the promise" refers to civil society's ongoing commitment to provide, via education, a universal path to dignity and success for all. Our use of the phrase "the institution of education" is deliberate; it is a loaded phrase that we feel captures a variety of cultural, social, and economic constructions surrounding skills and "academic capability." The institution of education also refers to journeys of individual and collective growth, in which a set of fixed metrics and measurements is used to label and facilitate "achievement." It is a concept we use to address how, both locally and globally, people are instructed and later encouraged to follow a pathway through schools, colleges, and universities that will put them in the "best" position to claim an appropriate citizen status whilst simultaneously measuring their contribution to the labor market. In other words, we are talking about how we learn, the institutions that socially reproduce this, and the cultures that protect the process. As this book is focused primarily on neurotypical hegemony, we are specifically concerned with how we consent to the institution of education but also, and crucially, with how it can be resisted.

While we use the politics of neurodiversity to bring some fresh perspectives to contemporary discussions about the cultures that the institution of education normalizes, we see this chapter as very much embedded in the work of our fore parents such as Paulo Freire, bell hooks and Stuart Hall, who so often spoke of the liberatory and emancipatory freedoms education can provide. In short, there are pockets of hope in how we use existing scholarship to help us to imagine new directions in education. In this way, our reflections on the institution of education and the politics of neurodiversity lay the foundations for the landscape in which we work through these issues. Here in the UK, we are located in the belly of the Empire, where many of the beliefs that sought to justify the theft of land and enslavement through colonial expansion were intellectually localized. We need look no further than the continued impact of twentieth century eugenicists. Knowledge producers such as Francis Galton provided many of the ideological grounds for theories of "racial improvement" and "planned breeding," which stated that so-called social ills were the result of genetics and heredity. Robert Chapman has stressed that the intellectualization of what would become known as race science and eugenics still influences "public understanding, policy, and clinical practice relating to neurodiversity to this very day."[2] The intellectualization of racism and ableism has informed a systemic production of difference which has been integral to the way civil society reproduces itself. This process relies on many different collaborators, but the construction of the institution of education continually demonstrates that it is a key player in this process.

Returning to REM's imaginary Great Beyond, we affirm that this mythical location of academic excellence is an empty promise that takes us away from collective cohesion and har-mony—it separates us and pulls us apart. In some ways, the Great Beyond is about reaching for something we are told is achievable, regardless of our positionality. The lyrics of "The Great Beyond"—*I'm pushing an elephant up the stairs / I'm toss-ing out punchlines that were never there / over my shoulder a piano falls . . . / crashing to the ground*—begin to capture the essence of what we are seeking to explore in this chapter. The pressures of the institution of education on all people—even those whose path is understood as more linear and straightforward—fail us all and are a part of our culture that keeps a neurotypical hege-mony of intellect in place. This is an integral part of our argu-ment for many reasons, and our style of persuasion in the way we write about these matters locates the political as the per-sonal and neurodivergent as a prelude to our collective, Black, neurodivergent, and subjective engagement with the institution of education in this chapter. Thus, we are diving back into the cultural and social ways in which neurotypical hegemony comes to exist within the ether.

These are academic terms that have largely been created in community with others,[3] and though we see them as essential tools for articulating visions of social justice, we feel that it would be useful for all readers to offer a reminder of what we are talking about.

What Do We Mean by the Institution of Education?

The institution of education relates to the relationships and structures that form the basis of how we are told to learn. It pre-sents the idea that education is something which is engaged in at a set time, and in a set location. It is built around values that have become fixed on markers and algorithms of achievement that are deemed universally applicable to all people. We draw on the concept of the institution of education to highlight the connection between the way teachers are trained, classrooms are constructed, and social relationships generated in them, as an idea that encapsulates the social reproductions that inform the present-day learning environment. The institution of education is *a culture* that relies on a vast set of ideas which condenses nearly every aspect of modern civil society—the set-text books, thirty people in a classroom or more than eighty in a lecture theatre; hours of homework; detention, punishment and isolation; solo working, timed examinations and the idolization of league tables of schools and universities. The institution of education encapsulates the idea that the best and most valuable learning occurs as a solo project of comprehension in which the subject we are learning is taught by another person, an educator or teacher. Every aspect of much of our global institution of education is benchmarked; learners are compared on the basis of "passing," "failing," or "requiring more support." The timed and written exam has become the cornerstone of these habitual rituals. There are of course exceptions to this, globally, but we are in the business of outlining hegemony, which by its very nature is about what becomes powerful and dominant. While we seek to draw on some of the more positive demonstrations of inclusive and emancipatory education, the urgency of these matters requires us to lay bare just how much our society relies on the institution of education to keep racism, ableism, and capitalism firmly in place.

The institution of education is one of the primary sites at which neurotypical hegemony becomes normalized among young people, families, and teachers. It later becomes a phenomenon that follows us throughout our lives as a signifier of value or a reminder of how educational achievement became one of the primary ways in which our sense of self is hindered. We see the outliers to these processes as a continuous source of hope. As bell hooks notes, these are the teachers located in educational settings who transgress the boundaries that confine students to an "assembly line approach" and see the possibilities of self-growth (of the teacher) as inextricably linked to resisting what we have been told is the "right" way to educate.[4] Returning here to the tension between structure and agency, one can see how the institution of education—in spite of all its pitfalls—can also be a culture where resistance is created in the everyday. People have the capacity in these spaces to use their agency and understanding of the society we live in to make clear that a lack of affiliation with the way we are told to "learn" does not negate your value as a human being. The fact that you find physics, phonetics, or science very challenging does not mean you are not worthy of a dignified life. It is, as bell hooks notes, the teachers who transgress who have the power to show that young people or adults deserve love, even if they are rejected by a school. Not only do you still deserve love, you deserve for your creativity to flourish and be nurtured. You still deserve ordinariness, even if you struggle to communicate your passions. Our current educational culture and its measured and measurable outcomes continue to question notions of humanity and value.

The tensions between structure and agency explored in chapter 2 illustrate just how the institution of education becomes one of the main ways we understand people and difference, as well showing how individuals produce a sense of self. A sense of self is an identity and acceptance of oneself. It is a site at which civil society is intimately produced. Many of the threads in this chapter link directly to the arguments we addressed in chapters 2 and 3, concerning love and mental health, masking, and ED or the ways in which we avert our minds, refusing to focus on matters that cause us harm. This is why we must take seriously the power of education, and how it becomes a primary conduit for neurotypical hegemony.

School and Subjectivity: Reflections on Education

When we were writing this book, *everything* came back to education. This is partly because we are educators, but also because our Black subjectivities—that is, our experiences and understandings of ourselves—were very much formed and marginalized by school. Simply put, we found it hard to discuss the relationship between neurotypical hegemony and education in neutral terms. Like many Black, and Black and neurodivergent, children, our time in education was loaded with racism by way of anti-Blackness and ableism, and each of us brought to the conversation our lived experiences as young people and adults. We are also academics who specialize in education, drawing on the ways in which structures of gender, race, and class specifically breach efforts to create equitable outcomes across a student's life cycle. Because of this, we draw on the sociologies of education of scholars such as David Gillborn, who has dedicated much of his career to research that documents the ways in which negative racialization, and racism specifically, are operationalized in schools.[5] Gillborn notes the integral nature of structure and agency in education but stresses that is it the cultures of white normativity, a common and historically informed projection of young people of color as educationally inferior, and the way these kinds of cultures become embedded both subtly and overtly in education policy, that remain integral. Rereading together Gillborn's extensive scholarship on racism in schools took us back to our own experiences of school and the subtle ways in which our sense of self was subverted, not only because of a lack of connection to the way people are learning, but also because of the way race is subject to educational expectations. In Gillborn's words, education policy is not designed to eliminate racism but is actually in place to sustain it. Drawing on our own experiences of schooling, we assert below that to sustain itself, racism relies on ideological consent to neurotypical hegemony across the whole institution of education. For us, the relationship to neurotypical hegemony and the global institution of education is about how these exceptionally large cultures (places) become embedded in processes that have the capacity to take young people away from their passions, creativity, and drive to learn. As bell hooks states, we are made to believe that the classroom is a democratic space where our structural differences are resolved through a universal desire to learn.[6] The fact that such myths around the universal and cohesive nature of the institution of education endure makes it urgent to take a more cautionary, as well as a more direct, approach in this chapter. These are big issues, which find their way to groups and individuals who are already at the sharper end of inequality more broadly, and we address them through the politics of neurodiversity, or by looking more closely at how norms and assumptions about ways to learn become socially reproduced through rigid notions of how to be educated. Loving frameworks remain at the heart of our delivery—but readers will certainly notice a shift of tone in how we talk about education, perhaps because like bell hooks we see education as one of the clear ways in which society reinvents its hierarchies as the natural order of things rather than seeing them as cultures that in many ways have been intentionally curated.

Chantelle:

For Chantelle, a combination of coming of age in a predominantly white suburban town with several undiagnosed neurodivergent traits, and simultaneously trying to adhere to the demands of education, made school challenging:

> I often felt I had a great deal of enthusiasm but very little space to channel it in a way that was conducive to mainstream education. Sitting down for longer than fifteen minutes felt agonizing, and in the afternoons all I wanted to do was sleep. I was a poor reader, but a confident speaker; I had bad reading comprehension, but a well-developed understanding of how to make people feel good through words.

In these initial reflections from Chantelle, we begin to align our perspectives on school with much of the existing literature, in relation to the connection between race, ableism, and gender—for Black girls in particular. While disability has not been at the forefront of her scholarship on education, we lean into the teachings of seminal scholars like Heidi Mirza, who note that in spite of the ongoing racialization and gendered exclusion of Black girls in school, they still find ways to thrive outside the parameters of teachers' low expectations.[7] This was very much the case in Chantelle's experience, as she notes the impact of ableism on being able to be intellectually present in school, as well as her ability to *find a way* "by making people feel good." Generally speaking, school is very complicated for neurodivergent girls. They are taught to be passive and constantly positioned in opposition to "naughty" boys. So often, these naughty boys are the ones labelled as, or diagnosed with, ADHD. For Chantelle, "this meant everyday repression of how my brain really wanted to function." And like many other girls, the consequences were that we were unable to engage in learning in ways that felt natural and kind to ourselves.

Jason:

For Jason's mother, Gifty, who was his staunch advocate, as well as for his sense of self, mainstream education was an ongoing battle. Being non-verbal until the age of eleven and not being able to read or write until he was eighteen years old meant that the institution of school was beyond difficult: "I was labelled, ignored, hyper visible and excluded all at once." In the prevailing conditions of 1980s and 90s Britain, it was near impossible for Black families whose children had special educational needs (SEN) to be treated as human, let alone in loving and dignified ways. These formative experiences of education led us towards lives in which we have fought for our ways of learning to be taken seriously, and—regardless of our school-measured ability—to break new ground in higher education. This battle has always been a very real phenomenon. For us, the great beyond has been about getting other people to recognize that our creative and neurodivergent ways of teaching and learning are as valuable as an A grade in maths. Our experiences have shown us the glaringly obvious nature of the institution of education, which, while being in our opinion incredibly difficult to contest, would also be the easiest to dismantle.

The urgency faced by neurodivergent young people and their families, in relation to schooling especially, is well documented amongst clinical psychologists and social scientists. While a variety of interventions related to SEN schooling and other sensory, physical, and more cultural interventions, have sought to make schools more inclusive in general (and we see these positive moves on a global scale), the connection between the ideological and the psychological, through school especially, can show how identities become transcribed through ways of being, in relation to the combination of our differences and the institution of education. Scholars such as Sophie Connolly, Hannah Constable, and Sinéad Mullally see the impact of school distress and unmet needs on neurodivergent young people as among the biggest challenges facing advocates for more inclusive education and outcomes for all young people. We want to point out here the capacity for society to reproduce this situation of urgent need as normal in the cultures of civil society we inhabit. For example, the increasing number of neurodivergent children labelled "school refusers" comes to be understood as an inevitable outcome for groups who fall outside the parameters of value and normativity. What we mean here is that instead of examining the cultures that lead to school refusal, as a society we are constantly asserting that this is a consequence of young people being unable to fulfil the promises of neurotypical culture. The way this becomes individualized is a matter for us all, as the long-term effects of these educational outcomes have a lasting impact on how we care for all people in civil society.

School, Gender, and Neurodiversity

Throughout this discussion about how Black and neurodivergent subjectivity informs our view of society we have sought to embed in our analysis the ways in which this is (of course) mitigated by gender. As our reflective vignettes show, gender, race, and schooling bring to a head some of the key sites at which neurotypical hegemony divides and organizes those it must marginalize to reproduce itself socially. Gender becomes a conduit, reason, and mechanism that keeps the schooling element of the institution of education in place.[8] In this way, our understandings of masculinity and femininity in girls and boys are at the heart of what we want to explore in relation to education and neurodiversity. Neurodivergence has been understood as more noticeable in boys, but this does not mean that they have received more care. Similarly, the way girls and other genders become predisposed to being sidelined and ignored throughout school shows that this process eventually becomes a blueprint for others. By corroding and incrementally depressing the educational experiences of one group, we are effectively creating guidelines for the future management of other groups.

In school and in society, neurodivergent boys often come to understand their brains through shame, punishment, isolation, and hypervisibility.[9] Even when space is made for neurodivergent boys *to be themselves*, this will be—routinely—outside the mainstream school environment. In order to be themselves, neurodivergent boys are continually separated from their peers, further exacerbating their social isolation and reproducing the myth that neurodivergent people struggle socially.[10] We are drawing attention to neurodivergent boys in order to paint a picture of how the marginalization of boys further subordinates girls and other genders. In many cases, the only way for neurodivergent girls to be noticed is to engage in punishable behavior that mirrors the behavior of neurodivergent boys. This is why "disruption" becomes one of the only means by which a neurodivergent girl can compete with the hypervisibility of neurodivergent boys. Depending on where a girl sits on the spectrum, if there is a limit to their capacity to assimilate, they are more likely to be noticed or punished, or perhaps—in more positive cases—cared for. What we are saying is that, for neurodivergent people, school continues to be a cauldron of stigma, negativity, and marginalization. In the current system, in which class sizes are larger and support services staff are in short supply, drawing readers' attention to the way that everything—in the main—stays the same and reproduces itself, is crucial for recognizing how this all begins to map onto wider structures and cultures within the confines of the institution of education.

Returning to the intersection of race and gender in schools, Black boys are overexposed to a concoction of hypervisibility and invisibility, stratified by negative racialization, racist stereotypes, and the organizing principles of neurotypical hegemony.[11] Hypervisibility results in punishment, negative labelling, and isolation. Invisibility becomes embedded in an intrinsically felt negation of identity, worthiness, and value. Put simply, hypervisibility for Black men and boys has never been a good thing. Applying the lens of the politics of neurodiversity to this matter, we see how this experience in and of itself can be stretched towards other groups and people. Here, we speak to the reader directly and ask you to think about what it would mean to exist within an institution which by its very nature has positioned your sense of self as unworthy of love, learning, and growth. In this way, the gendered and racialized experience of Black boys in schools illustrates what has happened, what continues to happen, and what could happen to others. Here we utilize the wisdoms of the late, great Stuart Hall as a guide for illustrating the power of hegemony to alternate between groups as a way of maintaining power over the masses and our cultures.[12] It doesn't matter how much time passes, how much research we commit to exposing gendered anti-blackness, our grief—as Black educators—coalesces around the way Black boys especially experience the school system by emphasizing that it never stops being painful to use this experience as an example of inequality. But we use the example of Black boys to begin to do the intellectual work of showing exactly why these are matters for all of us. Here, we need to be looking critically at how gender, race, and class—and their structures—become synonymous with myths about educational ability. For neurodivergent boys, for example, much of their development, including of their sense of self, takes place alongside the stigmatization of their neurodivergent traits: for them, the classroom has become a site of conflict in which neurodiversity has become something punishable. It is difficult to see the light when it comes to positioning neurodiversity beyond the confines of punishment but for us, hope lies in the deconstruction of everything we think we know about learning.

Teacher Training

Of course, integral to these issues around schooling, gender, and neurodiversity are the educators, teachers, and leaders of learning. Here in Britain and on a global scale the way teachers and educators are trained and instructed has undergone seismic changes. There are pockets of hope in relation to these changes. Take for example, the Welsh Government's recent direction to teachers, who must now ensure that Black and Asian Minority Ethnic education is included in all school curriculums.[13] But generally speaking, rapid changes in technology, global emergencies such as the COVID-19 pandemic, and more critical discussions about how we learn have created a turbulent decade for the teaching profession at all stages. Multiple changes have required teacher education providers, trainees, and in-service teachers to pivot continually on the whims of whichever education secretary is incumbent at the time. The multiethnic, diverse, and complex needs of pupils now require schoolteachers to be able to adopt a myriad of pedagogical approaches. A more recent criticism of teacher preparedness has been the historical focus solely on pedagogy and behavior. Navigating and accommodating a classroom full of children with a variety of differences and needs is now a compulsory and integral part of the modern teacher's armory. At the same time, the existence of neurodivergence in the classroom has become something with which teachers in mainstream schooling are struggling to cope, due to a variety of issues relating to resources, as well as the already-mentioned changing nature of society. While we do our best to ensure that we are de-individualizing our understanding of the ways in which neurotypical hegemony endures, we feel that some teachers seem predisposed to characterize neurodivergent pupils as "intellectually challenged," "slow," or "disruptive." And with this, teachers are often at risk of upholding the deficit mechanisms that are frequently used to forecast attainment outcomes (which frame much of the institution of education). The gradual erosion of confidence that is a consequence of this is also partly facilitated by the classroom environment created by the teacher, on the instruction of the powers that assert the importance of the neurotypical framing of learning. The instruments needed to create a multidimensional classroom environment for neurodivergent people are admittedly not easily acquired. Teachers need to be supported; there should not be penalties for innovative pedagogues, who need autonomy within overarching educational systems to engage with modes of assessment and learning that go beyond the confines of key performance indicators.

The exclusionary classroom has facilitated an educational apartheid that attempts to differentiate between the able and "disabled." The universal approach to education generally requires pupils to assimilate, and failure to do so is used as a barometer of academic prowess. Policy-makers, thought-leaders, and educators need to think differently about how we train aspiring teachers, as well as how we support the continuing professional development of incumbent teachers, with regard to re-imagining and disrupting universal approaches that disadvantage those with specific learning needs. Rethinking education is particularly difficult, given the continual financial restrictions and pressures on educational institutions, the economic consequences of which have directly resulted in oversized classes with less practical support or fewer interventions. It is teachers who are on the front line of the social and material pressures of inequality. While we can see how more work on both disability and racial literacy is required amongst the teaching profession, this is a clear demonstration of how a lack of resources and support affects individual agency and thus one's ability to provide loving spaces for growth and learning of all young people.

Thematizing the Institution of Education

Readers will have noticed that our rebellion against traditional modes of communicating is embedded throughout the book, and that we have tried not to be too prescriptive about the order of matters. Of course, when mapping the institution of education we might be expected to talk about primary, secondary, college, higher, and further education in that order. But as with the rest of our analysis, we want to refrain from contributing to literature concerned with what is "bad," to look more at how structures of society become normalized, and how this produces cultures that directly and indirectly harm those more likely to be on the margins of society (although we should also acknowledge here the many among our neurodivergent and disabled siblings who find the current environment of education and its institutions straightforward). And in returning to the notion that civil society and hegemony rely even on those who are more likely to experience the sharper end of inequality to maintain the order of things, we mitigate and move beyond individualistic takes on social issues—especially important in something as crucial as education—by centering our discussion of the social reproduction of neurotypical hegemony in a way that draws on themes rather than chronologies. Education is a clear example—among other examples throughout the book—where we can show that its structure limits everyone in society. This is why it is essential to go beyond the neurodivergent individual, as there are many instances across history and contemporary society where the trajectories of neurodivergent people are used to solidify the current educational system and resist change.

The idea that skill, intelligence, and capability can only be properly measured by pre-designed exams is a key component of the modern institution of education, to which governments across the globe have consented. When we talk about the institution of education, we are talking directly about the protection and celebration of a particular set of metrics, a system of measurements of skill. The ways in which these are designed, delivered, and consented to are the key issues here. Across the book so far, our aim has been to demonstrate that to dismantle neurotypical hegemony, we must meet people where they are. As we try to understand the limits of neurotypical hegemony, we are clear that intentional political education needs to be democratized in a way that recognizes the fluidity of experience. Fundamentally, many "succeed" within the institution of education, even our disabled and neurodivergent siblings. But the fact that a particular form of learning is the benchmark for all achievement limits our imagination and the quest for progressive societies.

This is where we see the value of looking at the institution of education as separate but overlapping entities (and institutions).

We see these overlapping entities as educational beliefs, or rather as the shaping of these by—variously—the institution of education, leaders, algorithms, and the desire to be educationally "normal."

The Social Construction of Educational Beliefs

Among our communities and peers, and the other people we meet through school, work, and life, there is a tendency to reproduce a collection of ideas and values about education. Education is seen as the stepping stone to a dignified and ordinary life and it is up to individuals and their support networks or families to mobilize both their capabilities and the resources around them. Even among our own families and friends, we see these ideas being reproduced. The matter at hand is huge, but we know that committing to this challenge will harness a freedom that will structurally, spiritually, and practically liberate us all. What if we said that we have choices about the way we understand education and the concept of achievement? It is within our control to change our shared beliefs and values. By taking time, in this chapter, to outline the ways in which we see neurotypical hegemony as obstructing our ability to make different choices and build new educational cultures, we contribute to the plethora of existing research and scholarship that has shown that metrics, measurement, and the protection of a particular mode of learning limits our society's ability to nourish and evolve a diverse range of people and experiences.[14] The ability to perform well in exams should not result in the idolization of particular citizens, and by contrast, performing badly in school and education does not mean you are not worthy of a loving and dignified life.

When it comes to education and its institutions, there are shared sets of local and global beliefs and values. Our cultures consistently tell us that some people have "ability" and "skill," whereas others are simply not able to reach a satisfactory standard of academic attainment in accordance with the rest of the school-age population. This is such a fixed culture of beliefs in education that even as we write, we find ourselves hesitating about whether we can truly say that there is an appetite to resist this culture. Of course, we know of organizations that are pushing against these dichotomies, but it would trivialize the scale of the battle we face if we were to suggest that these movements have penetrated the bubble of education and academic excellence more broadly. There are some important standpoints here, that we can draw on with the help of our Black feminist siblings, who note that the way we understand education as a society so often determines who deserves to have access to the support that garners a strong and confident sense of self. Those who are positioned as deserving of an education that suits their ways of learning come to rely on a hierarchy of what has been considered valuable, useful, and intellectually astute. For us, this is also one of the parameters of love, and of the question of who gets to be considered worthy of the institution of education. Here, we draw attention to the fact that our culture allows only some people to make mistakes—to go through the back door, pick themselves up and start again—whereas others get to experience what can only be described as institutional refuse. Similarly, we see this process as exemplifying the combination of Gramsci and Hall's hegemonic condition. When it comes to how our beliefs about education, or the institution of education, become embedded, we must continue to pay attention to the people whose experiences it routinely rejects. Hegemony, and in this case neurotypical hegemony, relies on their participation as well as on the societal justification of their marginalization. This, we argue, is structural, but also depends on the ways our educational beliefs become part of how we relate to each other. Those at the sharpest ends of marginalization are required to believe that they are either partly or entirely to blame for their lack of assimilation into the institution of education.

The core belief we want to expose and eventually abolish is measurement by way of exams. In our ever-changing society, we feel it is no longer reasonable, useful, or beneficial to measure anyone's educational ability through a fixed set of exams. We join the many before us who are now actively choosing a side on this matter. John Hannah, the director of Student Affairs Special Projects at Ryerson University in Toronto, stated that one of the core reasons for diminished student well-being and mental health in contemporary learning environments relates directly to our systemic reliance on and adoration of the exams system.[15] In England and Wales for example, we have a very odd education system where school exams usually take place in May and June and results are awarded in August. Secondary school children in particular are given a surplus of information that they are required to remember and regurgitate, typically during a silent ninety-minute exam. In some cases, these exams can be two hours or longer. Families are told that their children must take their exams as an essential part of their journey towards proving their value in society. Framing exams and their results in this way transcends academic value and becomes reproduced as the first key milestone at which an individual must prove their worth and productivity.

For educators reading this, we understand that there are a number of reasonable objections to the notion that we should abolish all measurements and metrics and key performance indicators. How will we sort people? How will we measure skill? How will the "best" people get to be in charge of things? In the first instance, in response, we would like to address two key starting points. In order to produce hopeful visions, we have to believe that most of our readers—whether they are educators or people with a general interest in our arguments—are capable of changing their minds about the cultures produced by neurotypical hegemony or are already in support of the changes we wish to argue for. We have to believe that people can change their minds. On this point in particular, we draw on the ways our beliefs are constructed as a way to point to the flaws of the current system and the clear opportunities for a combination of both inclusion and freedom in changing it. In chapter 7, we return to the abolition of the exam system as an essential component of our manifesto for dismantling neurotypical hegemony.

While the tension between structure and agency, and what this means for the politics of neurodiversity, is something we keep returning to, we need to pay close attention—in the case of how beliefs about education become socially constructed—to the ways in which people use their agency to set the agenda within the institution of education. Part of this is connected to the commitment to neurotypical hegemony and the belief that it organizes society equitably. To dismantle it requires an appreciation of the different roles we all play in this movement. We are told that governments administer the will of the people. Crucially important here are the leaders who teach us how things should be, or what is best for everyone. Leaders exist in all institutions, as well as in our families. They are the people who reinterpret the values, morals, and beliefs that begin as the will of the people and go on to be enacted by local authorities and government. But as we have argued in our discussion so far, the will of the people is strongly differentiated (and unevenly distributed) according to class, race, gender, nation, and of course neurodiversity. The task at hand is to generate ideas and philosophies that recognize the tensions between the universal and the particular in the ways that educational institutions reproduce notions of learning, and in the model of education itself. Although there is a tendency to protect and preserve the neurological hierarchy in educational institutions, we can still see that not all people everywhere are committed to beliefs that marginalize other ways of being and knowing in education. This is where the opportunities for resistance and reimagination can be found. We need to hold onto the idea that although there is a struggle for power, people do not willingly malign others based on outdated conceptions of educational achievement (see also chapter 6).

Those tasked with administering the beliefs and values we associate with educational institutions are required to produce particular outcomes for schools and universities, and in doing so are often producing ideas and cultures that subvert the needs of those who fall outside the definition of (or at least, what is counted as) academic excellence. Those who are negatively impacted by these cultures are offloaded, negatively labelled, and in some cases removed altogether. This process falls directly into line with the pressure on leaders in education to uphold neurotypical hegemony. It is therefore necessary to rethink our belief systems, values, and the abolition of performance indicators.

When Algorithm Meets Aspiration

Neurodivergent individuals' desire to learn is capped from an early age by various forms of deficit messaging that feed the prevailing discourse that they are somewhat inadequate. Much of this is mapped against how we define intelligence in educational spaces, resulting in a culture and attitude that renders disposable individuals who may exhibit or enact their intelligence through different mediums. The dismissal of neurodivergent people in our education system continues be consequential, especially with regard to the significant number of individuals who have gone through the system without a diagnosis of their underlying and potentially neurodivergent traits. Many disability rights activists assert that some of the clearest examples of the intersectional struggle, of neurodivergent young people in particular, can be found in schooling. At the time of writing, as we outlined at the beginning of the book, our home country is experiencing a crisis in the cost of living, in which families with disabilities are some of the hardest-hit. We point to this example to illustrate the way that class insecurity can be exacerbated by disability and negative labelling in education (see chapter 5). And of course, the terrain of a civil society bound to racism, ableism, and capitalism makes the institution of education all the more challenging for neurodivergent people. Black children must grapple with the past but incredibly pertinent issue, described by Bernard Coard as a label of educational subnormality, in which entry into the institution of education fuses with negative racialization (or anti-blackness) to create a culture of intellectual marginalization (see Afterword).[16] Looking more closely at what this means for Black children who are also neurodivergent, we see a combination of proximity to isolation, punishment, adultification, and a more general suppression of their creativity. This is of course mapped onto the gendered formations of race and ableism, where we know that Black girls are at higher risk of missing their diagnoses. And while we are discussing only the example of Black children at this point, we recognize that these matters remain multiclassed and multiethnic. As sociologists concerned with social justice, but also love, we feel the issue is that despite the way the conditions of the institution of education create algorithms of educational worthiness, so many of our siblings still have an intrinsic desire to fit

in, be successful, and prove to educators that they have aspirations and are able to assimilate. This in itself is about how a love
of oneself can be thwarted by external algorithms that are designed to sort people into groups of educational worthiness,
which then have the capacity to become a guiding principle for
how we see ourselves as individuals.

While this chapter involves a political commentary on the
ways in which the institution of education is a key pillar of
the social reproduction of neurotypical hegemony, we must
contend with the fact that we live in a society where ideas about
educational achievement have the capacity to guide a person's
life trajectory in its entirety. While we see the intersection of
race and class here as integral to recognizing just how urgent
these matters can be for the neurodivergent learner, educational
marginalization is in no way an exact science. The title of this
section—*when algorithm meets aspiration*—is designed to acknowledge that despite the disproportionate marginalization
of neurodivergent people, we are still capable of finding ways to
achieve the desired outcomes. Often, we see how those unable
to achieve (what is conventionally perceived as) "success"
are positioned as apathetic or simply as unable to participate in
the process of learning. In this way, the educational aspirations
and intellectual capability of neurodivergent individuals have
often been the focus of forensic assessment by educational psychologists and psychotherapists. The history of these algorithms is one of embedded eugenicist ideas about neurology
and ability, stratified by race, class, gender, and of course, nation. Algorithms and aspirations become synonymous with
those who are seen as productive and valuable. Crucially, this
history transcends age, and disabled adults as well as children
are cruelly subjected to its constraints. Since we contend that
to liberate everyone the removal of these algorithms is essential,

it is imperative to be clear that many of them are based on an acquired expertise that is largely subjective.

Given the complexity and dexterity of the human brain, the fact that we live in a society where the assessment of an individual's cognitive abilities can be predicated on algorithms that we know to be harmful and reductive should be a cause for concern for all social justice movements. Part of us recognizes that disrupting neurotypical hegemony also requires us to assert the power of our individual agencies and capacities to adapt and respond, regardless of neurological difference. Prescribing the "correct" parameters of educational achievement limits the horizons of teaching and learning; the brain's adaptability and ability to respond to stimuli provides us with a framework to assert that in loving and understanding environments, with reasonable and inclusive adjustments, all individuals can develop and harness their learning.

The Desire for Education

Much of our academic careers have been spent advocating for more equitable outcomes in education. At the time of writing, we have more than twenty years' experience between us, of spending hour upon hour speaking to mainly well-meaning people across the education sector about the existence of institutional racism and how to eradicate it from our schools and universities. Along with many others who have for decades fought for change across the education sector, our aim has been to find ways to extract resources from institutions, as well as making the case for equity and inclusion for all our marginalized siblings. We are of the school of thought that prioritizes a vision of social justice at the epicenter of education. Put simply, everyone should have access to the possibilities, choices, and freedoms that knowledge is able to provide. A social justice lens recognizes the elitism that haunts our spaces, as well as the slavery and exploitation that built them.

The last thirty years have seen a significant increase in the number of students progressing to higher education, particularly from multiethnic, working-class backgrounds. Given the turbulent nature of the educational life course, and the fact that individual experiences of education vary depending on the environments people encounter, it is important to establish what affects educational desire. Often, the motivation to acquire more education is instrumental, and stems from an ambition to become socially mobile, as education has often been linked to social and economic capital. Looking closely at the long-term impact of algorithms and educational aspirations produces a clear-cut exemplification of the connection between class and ableism. The fact that ours is a society where "experts" judge intellectual ability according to a fixed set of education milestones remains a concern not just for disabled people, but for everyone. This is because these measurements have the capacity to thwart an individual's ability to be themselves, to be creative and tap into what it means for them to contribute to this world. As we have already emphasized, these education milestones benefit a minority but also exist in the service of neurotypical hegemony.

The wider implications of this for neurodivergent individuals entering higher education include clear disadvantage and a subsequent paralysis of educational desire and ambition. In most cases a lack of financial capital can also affect access to required support, resources, and infrastructure, especially when an individual's neurodivergence has been missed at earlier stages of education. The confidence derived from positive educational experiences (or the lack of confidence that stems from their absence) becomes a springboard for how we physically and mentally associate with, or disassociate from, education. The nature of higher education has historically been based on a narrow definition of intellect and intelligence that often ostracizes those who do not fit into this restrictive and exclusionary sphere. For individuals diagnosed with a neurodivergent trait as an adult, this can be incredibly disorientating. The subsequent and inevitable juxtaposition involves a sense of validation and understanding, while at the same time exacerbating feelings of frustration, anger, and resentment towards the education system. This clash of feelings inevitably affects the desire to learn, and we know that failure has economic consequences that rarely take into consideration either the circumstances that have affected academic attainment and progression, or the enforced assimilation required for neurodivergent people to progress through an exclusionary neurotypical system. The agency required to disrupt these spaces is something that should ordinarily be instilled in people throughout their educational journey, but can become quite difficult to acquire, since so much of it is underpinned by access to various forms of capital.

Concluding Remarks

As with many of our thoughts about civil society throughout this book, the message of this chapter is one that is both political and personal. It is not that we believe we have all the answers but that we can see a culture which so often feels impenetrable. And without trying to reinvent the wheel, we just want to make clear that things need to change, and that we see that change as directly linked to how we understand what learning is, what it is for, who it is for, and why it should be positioned as a right for all citizens. We are very aware of the global movement of

teachers, educators, and social justice activists that continues
to generate new visions for more equitable learning spaces and
access to knowledge, but these are not the people we are speaking to. The people we are speaking to are on the cusp of recognizing that things need to change. This change is holistic, in that
it covers both childhood and adulthood learning and access to
knowledge. In this way, we see that a culture centered around
the abolition of metrics, algorithms, and exams will help us to
truly change how we understand value, human life, and ultimately everyone's ability to access an ordinary and dignified life
in a way that centers their creativity, passion, and sense of self. Some
may come away from this chapter with the feeling that they
need more facts. The facts about the educational achievement
of disabled young people, in particular, are all out there. We live
in a society with a tremendous amount of access to information. Our job as sociologists concerned with the structures of
society and how these interact with agency is to make a cultural
argument that speaks directly to the individual in relation to the
structures we are all navigating. Simply, it is no longer enough
for us to tell you that the institution of education needs a complete overhaul; all we can do is show you how neurotypical hegemony affects the whole of society.

5

A Design for Life

RACE, CLASS, AND NEURODIVERSITY

Libraries gave us power
Then work came and made us free
What price now
For a shallow piece of dignity
(MANIC STREET PREACHERS, 1996)

THE MANIC Street Preachers are a Welsh rock band who have spent most of their careers producing consciousness-raising music and lyrics about the lives of ordinary people. The quote above, from the song "A Design for Life," explores the tension between capitalism and education. The way for us to gain dignity and control of our lives, they suggest, is to gain an understanding of our position as humans and workers. But as with our provocations in chapter 2, the introductory lyrics for this chapter relate to the fact that it is our material conditions and the space we are given to understand the world around us that often controls how we think about society. This space, we argue in this chapter, is highly dependent on networks and resources. Access to money and networks has a demonstrable impact on a disabled and neurodivergent person's capacity to manage an ableist society. Our analysis of class and neurodiversity—from both material and humanist perspectives—acknowledges that *just* recognizing neurodivergence or disability is not enough for a politics that centers social justice for everyone. As you read through this chapter, we would like you to focus on and imagine the experience of both neurotypical and neurodivergent working-class people who are struggling to feed themselves and their families, heat their homes or find a career path that fulfils them. Many of these people are working multiple jobs or are pushed out of careers due to the dominating cultures of neurotypical hegemony. Though we recognize that these cultures are not new and that class inequality is an inherent part of capitalist society, we feel it is necessary to emphasize the particularly pernicious nature of this conjuncture in the face of such huge concentrations of wealth, alongside the sustained existence of poverty on a global scale. It is always important to flag that degrees of impoverishment vary greatly by location. This can be traced, by and large, to the geographies of global north and south. And while our ambition is to focus on the lives of those who are experiencing the sharper end of class inequality, we also believe that the consequences of capitalist formations can negatively affect the lives of those who benefit materially from these cultures. We will address the fact that access to resources makes life more liveable, but even those who experience a more straightforward relationship with capitalism have a role in the reproduction of a culture that socially reproduces a lovelessness that impacts everyone. Although this might not be felt instantly, we contend that if one group is able to live more liveable lives at the expense of the marginalization of others, social and cultural repercussions develop both structurally and interpersonally for everyone. For instance, greed and the accumulation of resources on such a vast scale produces loveless cultures that find their way even into the lives and experiences of those who benefit most from them (how many very wealthy and unhappy people do you know). Here, we contend that there is a paucity of evidence that those who benefit materially from class inequity are entirely content. As we explored in chapter 3, a global mental health crisis is a multiclassed phenomenon. Lovelessness has a way of entering our lives and communities in a manner that impedes our sense of self and our journey towards self-actualization, which is something that goes beyond class. Ultimately, we are thinking here about how the interaction between structure and agency affects the way we see, accept, and love ourselves. We are also returning to the point that none of us are free until we are all free.

As with the other threads in this book, we bring together the lives of both neurominorities and neuromajorities as an example of how ableist cultures and practices generate a society grounded in the idea that our worth is connected to our relationship to labor and the workplace. Our exploration—in this chapter—of particular cultures and practices, aims to show that in order to dismantle neurotypical power, we need to understand the ways in which it permeates existing inequalities. One of the primary inequities that fuels ableism is that of class. To embed an inclusive politics of neurodiversity is to recognize that being neurodivergent or disabled does not automatically qualify us to understand the importance of material conditions, either for survival or for the provision of space to live dignified, ordinary, and fulfilled lives. In fact, many of us in the global neurodiversity community have benefited materially from the ways in which capitalism organizes our personal and professional lives (see later sections). But to center class and ableism is to make clear that this is one of the key aspects of social justice work and to imagine that it can help us all gain greater power over, and control of, our lives.

The connections between class and neurodiversity transcend the material needs of disabled people and their families. A class analysis of neurodiversity must take seriously the way ideological power becomes woven into the redistribution of resources. As we have outlined throughout the book so far, representation does not amount to freedom, and neurodiversity can itself be used to harness and tokenize particular populations and traits. Simply put, we have shown how being neurodivergent does not on its own produce a desire to dismantle neurotypical hegemony.

British Colonialism and the Making of Race, Class, and Capitalism

Much of our emphasis on naming the possibilities of neurodivergence as a way of seeing and understanding the world has been influenced by our siblings, who have pushed our imaginations through the theory, practice, and process of decolonial thought.[1] We are seeking to retrieve ways of knowing that stretch, obscure, and dismantle the fusion of neurotypical hegemony with the general whitening of how we come to know our lives.[2] Here, we are thinking about the ways in which histories of white (and European) dominance come to have a lasting ideological impact on how we live and relate to each other. In *Black Skin, White Masks*, Frantz Fanon discussed how his subjectivity (the way he saw and understood himself) as a colonized other became infiltrated by the politics of white assimilation. He was talking about what it means to come to understand a sense of self, or "who we are/ who one is" while living through the dominance of other groups. He noted that this caused self-fragmentation in ways that required the use of a "white mask" in order to get through the imposition of white social and cultural norms.[3] Fanon's timeless reflections on what it means to "live" marginalization while trying to reckon with how we get through and understand ourselves segues easily into a recognition of the importance of naming the continued impact of Empire and colonization on our more contemporary understandings of race and class. This then lends itself to an understanding of the way neurotypical hegemony becomes embedded in existing racialized and classed inequalities, which were formed through colonial domination. These histories are crucial for seeing how ways of knowing come to control the way we understand our social lives to this day. In relation to (what is considered) our modern understanding of the social order, or the question of which groups or individuals are considered valuable and human, we need to continue to return to conjunctures (or moments in history) like the imperialist and extractivist histories of slavery and colonial expansion, and the case of Britain's Empire, which laid the ground for the making of the local and global class antagonisms we see today.

As we began to introduce in chapter 4, we see the circumstances and ideologies that inform contemporary society as integral to the racialized and classed formations of neurotypical hegemony. These processes have been justified by an ideological force that embeds notions of purity and ableism, as well as the flimsy and changeable terrain of race. Some factual reflections on the impact of British colonialism, in particular, provide the basis for understanding how the formation of modern capitalism created conditions in which hierarchies of neurological, racialized, and classed difference could be understood as essential to the making of society. We see that neurotypical hegemony has produced cultures that have borrowed, taken, and repurposed much of the historical proliferation of racialized and classed inequality. Put simply, ableism is made possible through the histories of capitalism and colonialism.[4]

Race and Class at "Home" and "Abroad"

This section was inspired by the work of sociologists of race and class, including Imogen Tyler, Satnam Virdee, and James Trafford in particular. Their emphasis is on how a more thorough recognition of the role of internal colonization in the making of race and class (and ultimately, capitalism) can help to reconcile it with Empire, as a project not only of domination and extraction, but also of ideological control and alienation. Our historical thread here also takes inspiration from a keynote talk given by Chantelle and Imogen Tyler at The British Library (London, England) as part of the *Identities* journal annual conference in November 2022, titled "Living in the Wake of Colonial Capitalism: Racism, Poverty, Class Struggle." These reflections are also a nod to the inspirational work of American scholar of English Literature and Black Studies, Christina Sharpe.[5] What we are exploring here is how modern depictions of capitalism have their origins in Empire, the making of race and class, and the sorting of people or "subjects" as a means for profit.

Recognizing and reconciling what was happening in (home) imperial nations (in this case, Britain) while domination was occurring abroad provides greater insight into the version of postcolonialism we are currently negotiating in a society that appears to offer universal ideas about how we reach ordinary and dignified lives. We realize that we might sound repetitive here, but the history of all this is crucial. An understanding of how race and class becomes made 'at home' but also across the colonies is essential to understanding how capitalism creates systems of both economic and ideological control and domination. Capitalism continues to rear its head when we go more deeply into how harm and marginalization became justified through the 'need' for profit (we look at the history of this). As you read on, we encourage you to take stock of how the exploitation of a global and multiethnic working class (for profit) has been kept in place by practices of "divide and rule" across borders, which continues to provide the groundings for the invention of categories and hierarchies of humanity.

In the case of British colonialism and the expansion of empire, expenditure on and investment in colonial rule was born out of the crisis of feudalism.[6,7] The home and imperial core of Britain could not provide enough for its citizens. We can go back as far as the fourteenth century to see how pressure on populations—informed by famines, wars, and the black death in particular—constituted the economic justification for colonization. Britain saw the Spanish and Dutch voyages to the Americas as possible points of access to others' lands.[8] We therefore understand the island of Britain and its empire as bearing the seeds of what would later become a multiethnic working class organized through the borders of colonial expansion but grounded in the division between slavery and indentured labor in the colonies and the industrialized working class at home, living and working in squalor.[9]

The founding of the first English colony in Virginia in 1607 marked the beginning of a complex relationship between class conflict, racism, and the emergence of capitalism across the United States and the Caribbean. Initially driven by a small number of wealthy English elites, this imperial expansion led to the arrival of the first African slaves in Virginia in 1619. Throughout the eighteenth century, the capture and enslavement of

Africans intensified as the number of slave traders, plantation owners, and government officials increased. Callous chattel slavery became a deeply entrenched system on plantations, where mortality rates were high. Those who survived the brutal voyage aboard British slave ships in the mid-eighteenth century often faced only five to ten more years of life on British sugar plantations. Later, Asians were also forced into exploitative systems of indentured servitude. As Stuart Hall famously noted, this process transformed "systems of classification" into instruments of power. In short, categories of humanity were created to capture, control, and exploit Black and Brown labor throughout the Empire.

Slaves in the US and Caribbean resisted oppression in a variety of ways, ranging from subtle acts of defiance to large-scale rebellions. On plantations, enslaved people often engaged in everyday forms of resistance, such as working slowly, feigning illness, breaking tools or sabotaging crops. These acts disrupted the efficiency of the plantation system and demonstrated enslaved people's refusal to submit completely to their masters' control. They also participated in armed rebellions. The most famous in the US include Nat Turner's Rebellion in 1831, where Turner led a group of enslaved people in a violent uprising that resulted in the deaths of around sixty white people.[10] In the Caribbean, large-scale revolts such as the Haitian Revolution (1791–1804) led to the overthrow of colonial rule and the establishment of the first Black republic.[11] Other significant uprisings occurred in Jamaica, Barbados, and Guyana, where enslaved people fought for their freedom and, in some cases, negotiated better conditions.

Religious gatherings, maroon communities (escaped slaves who formed independent settlements), and the preservation of African cultural practices were other ways slaves resisted and asserted their humanity despite the brutality of the plantation system.

Returning to the island of Britain, in *The Making of the English Working Class* (1963), social historian E. P. Thompson examined how the English working class was "made" during the period between 1780 and 1832. He describes how the Enclosure Acts, which privatized common lands, destroyed the working people's access to independent subsistence and forced many rural laborers off their land. This transformation left them with no choice but to migrate to urban centers, where they became a captive labor force, vulnerable to exploitation in the new factory towns. Stripped of their traditional livelihoods and subjected to harsh working conditions, this displacement ignited widespread resistance among the working class.

One significant form of rebellion was the Luddite movement, where workers, particularly in the textile industry, protested the introduction of machinery that threatened their livelihoods. From 1811 to 1816, Luddites destroyed machines in factories, targeting symbols of industrialization and resisting the capitalist forces that prioritized profits over their well-being.

Rural laborers also fought back against landowners through the Swing Riots of 1830, a widespread uprising across southern and eastern England.[12] Agricultural workers rioted, setting fire to hayricks and smashing threshing machines in protest against low wages, poor working conditions, and the enclosure of common land. These riots reflected the desperation of rural laborers and their desire to reclaim some form of control over their lives. Such acts of resistance, although ultimately suppressed by the government, were expressions of class consciousness and solidarity. They highlighted the growing divide between the wealthy landowning class and the increasingly impoverished working class.

Tyler describes how many working-class people in England were displaced from the land and forced to migrate, often overseas or across the British Isles, in search of work. For example, the Irish moved to North West England and the Cornish sought jobs in northern mines and mill towns. Industrializing Britain was characterized by class exploitation and premature death, with food riots in the eighteenth century led by women during periods of famine and rising food prices. These struggles helped working people to see themselves as a class with shared interests, fighting for better living and working conditions. Industrial society in England emerged through constant unrest and resistance, just as enslaved and indentured people rebelled against the British property-owning classes in the colonies. Our goal is not to equate the experiences of the British working class with those enslaved and oppressed in the colonies, but to examine how the system of "divide and rule" functioned "at home."

Caribbean historian Eric Williams has pointed out that by 1750, every trading and manufacturing town in England was connected to plantation slavery, and the profits from colonial trade were a major source of capital that financed welfare and the industrial revolution. The British Empire relied on extracting resources—human, economic, and material—from the colonies, alongside the subjugation of the working class in Britain. As exploited workers in Britain began to gain concessions, eventually leading to the development of the welfare state, the connection between these struggles became more evident. Crucially, these concessions were enabled by capital accumulation in the Empire, as well as the creation of racial and ethnic hierarchies. Before the ideological project of the "deserving" poor took full shape, there were moments when the struggles of the working classes across the Empire were more easily unified.

Among the possibilities that emerge from drawing together these very different histories of racialized and classed exploitation, we find hope in better understanding a multiethnic working class that was formed both on the island of Britain and in its colonies. The highly industrialized social transformation of Britain cannot be understood without recognizing its investment in the capture and enslavement of Africans. We should also take seriously the class antagonisms that took shape in what Trafford refers to as the internal colony of Britain.[13] Historians have subverted the possibilities of a more unified account of this modern history of race and class by noting, for example, that the political identity of a working class racialized as white was galvanized by its radical engagement with racial superiority. Among intellectuals such as John Cartwright, William Cobbett, and Richard Carlile, the process of abolishing slavery was criticized on the grounds of an English racial superiority grounded on the flimsy criteria of "whiteness," "deservingness," "intellect," and "work." These eugenicist and racist philosophies sought to radicalize exploited industrial workers and turn them against both enslaved black people in the Caribbean and US and unconverted free Africans. It is in this process, itself fuelled by the interests of the elite, that we can see the groundwork for the expansion of the racist and ableist ideologies that are integral to the making of neurotypical hegemony in its contemporary form.[14]

The assertion of racial superiority draws on social structures and constructions and is embedded in myths about the "ideal human." These myths are grounded in racialized, classed, gendered, and ableist "typifications" that can be used to wield power, create value (see chapter 5) and facilitate depictions of what it means to be deserving or undeserving.

If we dive into the last two hundred years' industrial and technological developments on a global scale, we can see not only how intrinsic neurodiversity has been to these massive local and global shifts in social and labor relations but also how often it has been silenced. With the politics of neurodiversity existing in the shadow of mass capitalist production, it is here that we can see it as something both utilized and maligned. In the creation of hierarchies of neurological functioning, the structures and formations of race and class were, and continue to be, fundamental. And of course, one cannot comprehend the capitalist society in which we live today without addressing the issue of the transatlantic slave trade and indentured labor. The surplus of resources and money acquired through the exchange of people involved a range of actors and collaborators. Here in Britain, as the transatlantic slave trade took shape, we began to see class used in a new way to justify the sale of human life as a capitalist formation. The creation of a slavery database at the Centre for the Study of the Legacies of British Slavery, at University College London, has enabled historians such as Catherine Hall to show that money acquired in Britain through the enslavement of people became a fundamental feature of nearly all its institutions. While Britain expanded its empire, "the home front" accumulated resources to create a culture and society with a huge divide between rich and poor, and a well-resourced class of people to govern, rule, and set the agenda. Conversely, Tyler has stressed the importance of recognizing that the formation of race and class during slavery can be seen as a key moment at which white working-class people in Britain began to acquire consciousness of their material reality, while still being committed to the idea that the distribution of capital was fair and equitable. We can see the formation of the global working class in both the cotton field and the cotton mills. Capitalism has always needed fluidity in the creation of its workforce.[15]

The power of hegemony in this analysis is clear; the categorization of human difference is justified at the expense of other groups. People are trying to survive a social order which by its very nature seeks to dominate, exploit, and isolate those least likely to achieve the status of deservingness. The hope here lies in the possibilities of neurodivergent subjectivity (ways of knowing beyond the confines of neurotypical hegemony) for a better understanding of these histories, as a way to push back against those who seek to obscure the realities of empire, slavery, and colonization that still impact our lives today. Our point here is that knowing this history and inserting it into our present day understanding of ourselves is central to the project of dismantling neurotypical hegemony.

The Simultaneous Nature of Race and Class

Race is the modality in which class is lived.[16] We draw here on the words and wisdom of Stuart Hall et al. to begin to produce a class analysis of neurodiversity that centers anti-racist futures. Race becomes synonymous with the making of class, and these formations are integral not just to the neurodivergent individual, but also to the maintenance of neurotypical hegemony. And as we have previously argued, understanding social formations through the lens of Black and neurodivergent subjectivity offers a way of understanding both race and class that emphasizes the possibilities of disability justice for futures grounded in multiethnic and multiclassed solidarity.[17] Our emphasis, by way of our lived experience of Blackness and neurodivergence, on the intensification of racism and ableism provides an introduction to the analysis that brings race, class, and disability into focus. For example, many of the material and social requirements of Black people who happen to be working class automatically cross ethnic boundaries, as they share many of their needs with other, non-Black, groups. Further, if we take the specific structural formation of anti-Blackness, we can see how its similarities with other processes of negative racialization can produce solidarities informed by difference, yet united by multiethnic similarities. For example, histories of surveillance and myths around violence can be understood alongside the global social production of islamophobia faced by our Muslim siblings, who are of course multiethnic.[18] As we take seriously different processes of class inequity, racism, and racialization we can see how an emphasis on disabled or neurodivergent subjectivity can introduce ways to link these lives into a fusion of cultures. The formation of race and class relies on the subversion of relatability between groups, and it is here that we see neurodivergence as offering hopeful possibilities for unification against a common adversary—the socially constructed and inequitable distribution of power, capital, and resources.

Neurodiversity as a Means of Production

We are very much encouraged and inspired by the work of our disabled and neurodivergent siblings, who have contributed to the neurodiversity movement in a way that inserts class consciousness and stratification into our imaginings of a more inclusive, collectivized, and emancipatory culture for all. In this way, scholars such as Adam Bagley have made clear that the way we communicate as a society is deeply rooted in the means of production and capitalist ideas of "progress." To retain its dominance, capitalism needs to be able to communicate with the masses in a variety of ways. The construction of how *we should* communicate in social life and how that translates into the way we work is of course deeply rooted in a respectability that seeks to keep things "in order."[19] Bagley notes that "class struggle" is now "the information struggle," which by its very nature is subverting and regulating the subjectivity of the neurodiverse community.[20] This is about neurotypical hegemony and how it maintains its dominance through the consent of the very people it marginalizes. But in order to produce a politics that goes beyond a call for representation (and while the marginalization of disabled people is a key element in the history of capitalism), we also need to engage in the very messy and complicated work of acknowledging that neurodiversity has been used as a mechanism to uphold and reproduce class inequality.

To see how this particular dynamic has played out, we must still pay close attention to the history of disability and neurodiversity as things that have been used to malign populations through atrocities such as state sponsored ethnic cleansing and eugenics. In 1930s Germany, the Nazis saw both the denigration and extermination of disabled people as "in the interest of the national community." They positioned and labelled them as "incapable" so that they had to be kept in institutions for their entire lives, wasting the tax dollars of people who are not disabled. Amanda Tink notes that the Nazis frequently described disabled people as "useless eaters," "empty human shells," and "life unworthy of life."[21] The interplay between capitalism, ableism and life itself was at its most shocking not only in the killing but also in the forced sterilization that was legalized in 1933 via the enactment of the Law for the Prevention of Offspring with Hereditary Diseases. Fast forward to present day Britain, where we turn to the tireless campaigning of disability rights activists who have shown that, since 2007, welfare reforms have been the cause of numerous deaths due to flaws in the government Department of Work and Pensions' (DWP) system of Universal Credit, Personal Independence Payment, and Work Capability

Assessment systems. Both the Disability News Service (particularly John Pring) and Healing Justice London (and especially China Mills) have worked with families and survivors to bring to the attention of a wider audience the way the state's bureaucratic violence chips away at the spirit, and mental and physical health of disabled people.[22] Crucially, the DWP has employed the capitalist ideas of work and value as justification for withdrawing the benefits and support of thousands of disabled people and their families. These matters have become systemic due to the department's failure to pay attention to the pattern of deaths of claimants whose benefits were partially or completely cut. According to Open Democracy, "An investigation by the National Audit Office (NAO) on the information the DWP holds on benefit claimants who ended their lives by suicide, found the DWP does not identify patterns between people's deaths, meaning that 'systemic issues which might be brought to light through these reviews could be missed.'" At the same time, the DWP asserted that its failure to provide information on the risk to claimants of current policy was "due to a lack of centralized record-keeping . . . [which] was too costly and not in the public interest."[23]

While the connections between ableism, capitalism, and death remain central to the disability and neurodiversity movement, we see this moment as an opportunity for us to take stock of the technological evolution of capitalism, bringing to the fore the way neurodiversity, in particular, can be used to uphold neurotypical hegemony while also reproducing structural inequalities. As recently as 2021, the Government Communications Headquarters (GCHQ, UK), an intelligence and security organization responsible for providing information to the government and armed forces of the United Kingdom), was actively recruiting "neurodiverse dyslexics."[24] We know that an integral feature of some of the aforementioned state harms inflicted on disabled people relies on the upholding of mechanisms across other government departments that are embedded in the process of surveillance and "security." Crucially, this is how hegemony works and continues to reproduce itself—by relying on the labor and participation of marginalized groups who can prove their value through participation in cultures of harm. Our provocations here are concerned with what it means for us to live in a society where the mechanisms used to control people come to rely on the work and participation of the very people it seeks to marginalize. In this way, we can identify how modern depictions of neurodiversity can be mobilized not just to uphold neurotypical hegemony, but also to depict a more evolved state of capitalist relations.

According to the Bank of America website, there should be more emphasis on providing jobs for neurodivergent individuals as they can "give companies and society a boost" with their "valuable, hard-to-find capabilities."[25] In contrast to this, the journalist Anna Wise reported in *The Independent* online in 2023 that "People with neurodivergences and mental health problems are being 'financially harmed' by banks and other financial services firms."[26] Wise noted that the technological advancement of banking and financial services has a significant impact on the experiences of vulnerable and disabled people. These two contrasting provocations on the banks carry a historical irony that must be named. The connection between private sector organization advertising that showcases neurodiversity as something to be celebrated, while—at least in the case of the banks—having received significant funds by way of slavery demonstrates how hegemony becomes an unquestioned but embedded aspect of culture.[27] Banks can assert a desire for neurodivergent people to participate in the means of production, while also harming disabled people through a lack of access and support. At the same time, they are at the center of the inequities of modern capitalism that stem from historical enslavement and extraction.

We are acknowledging, in this chapter, something that many of our siblings have recognized already—that capitalism can adapt to changing social conditions, beliefs, and values. Capitalism is complex, slippery, and clever. The role of the neurodivergent scholar in this instance is to make the point that a bank's creation of an employment scheme for neurodivergent people does not equate to the liberation of some of the most marginalized people in our movement. Crucially, this mode of representation from within the belly of capitalist endeavor can be imagined more freely if we address the fact that race, class, and the marginalization of disabled and neurodivergent people have been integral to the formation of the bank that now asserts that it *can care*. Returning to love, and to meeting people where they are requires us to recognize that some readers may well be thinking, "but equality and diversity initiatives in any organization are a positive step towards imagining and creating more equitable lives and futures." Our response is one of agreement and understanding. We do want life to be more liveable, and if our neurodivergent sibling wishes to work for a bank, this is of course their choice. And if this bank wants to be more understanding of their disability, then this is also positive in many respects. However, our thesis and the argument we are making throughout this book entail a spiritual engagement with critical consciousness-raising in order to communicate the fact that an equality and diversity scheme will not free us, especially when such organizations have been built on the subjugation of our positionality. Recognizing this fact in an intentional way begins to provide some introductory dialogues toward ideological emancipation from neurotypical hegemony. Noticing that this bank might genuinely care about equitable working processes can be true at the same time that it is true that this is a move that symbolizes the social reproduction of capitalism. We are not in the business of apportioning blame or of an overtly interpersonal analysis of capitalism in this instance but—because we do not wish to excuse the way neurotypical hegemony functions to preserve capitalism—we are very much focused on the need for a critical consciousness which approaches neurodiversity as something that requires a politics with an emancipatory and structural approach.

Class, Capital, and Neurodiversity

Neurotypical hegemony functions to preserve capitalism. Neurodiversity, both for the collective and for the individual, can be more straightforwardly negotiated in the cultures we are exploring if one has access to economic and social capital. Though part of our address to the reader draws on subjective reflections about neurotypical hegemony that transcend the impacts of structure, it is imperative to recognize that it is easier for us to understand our own neurodivergence in the contexts of neurotypical hegemony if we have been given space—provided by capital—in which to understand ourselves and wider society. Access to resources makes life just that little bit more manageable. While we want to make arguments that center neurodivergent futures as emancipatory for everyone, social class is clearly a structure that some members of neurominority groups are able to negotiate in a much more linear way than others. This dynamic is of course still influenced by neurotypical hegemony being a seemingly "unwelcoming" space for neurominorities, but what we know is that inequity can become more manageable with help and support.

Secondly, when thinking about how to dismantle neurotypical hegemony, and social inequality more broadly, we need to acknowledge that neurodivergence and class together create a complex dynamic that can hold back the achievement of an emancipatory politics for everyone. The spectrum and multifaceted nature of neurodivergence in general appears to confirm the existence of a seemingly innocent and benign individualism. The neurodiverse community contains many similarities and differences, and in our journey towards self-actualization we can— understandably—find ourselves consumed by how the culture we are navigating gets in the way of our own sense of self. If we happen to be neurodivergent and navigating this process and find spaces for freedom without intentionally engaging with the politics of class, our experiences can easily be used to tokenize us and defend this culture. Knowingly or not, some of us are able to negotiate our neurodivergence in a way that complements the capitalist formation and speed of production. Meanwhile, our siblings at the sharper end of class inequality find that the intersection of class with disability makes life simply unliveable (see also chapter 3). This example shows clearly how the voices of the most marginalized in our movement must take priority, as the sharper end of material insecurity provides much more information about a multitude of positionalities across society. It is not enough for us to have lived experience of marginalization in order to generate a culture of emancipation. Crucially, if we were to focus on neurodiversity alone, we would risk reproducing the class inequities that cause harm at both local and global scales. The similarities that bind neurominorities—and which also bind us all—need to be enough to show that if our siblings are struggling then we are all in trouble. Of course, we can see many examples across global celebrity culture where neurodivergence seems to be a way to contribute adequately to society—and yes—in some cases this gives an illusion of acceptance and peace (see chapter 1). But we stress that if neurotypical hegemony is able to co-exist with a more individualized depiction of neurodiversity (supported by class insecurity), then it is only a matter of time before this culture turns its back on the people it currently appears to accept.

While we make clear that race is the modality in which class is lived, and that the history of racial formation through capitalism is integral to the marginalization of neurodivergent people, for Black neurodivergents the cultures in which they mask, and to which they adapt, purge both their internalized self (identity) and their external position (class). With all this in mind, we finish this section by drawing on the classed positioning of some of our Black, white, and multiethnic neurodiverse siblings to stress that even with structural advantages gained through the cultures of capitalism and class inequity, marginality and isolation will still rear their heads unless we take everyone with us.

Capitalism and Liberalism

Between the twentieth and twenty-first centuries, capitalist formations and the means of production both grew and became more all-embracing. Capitalism's ideological legitimacy—or the means by which its existence is justified—has evolved alongside a psychosocial and collective culture organized around the idea of "bettering one's position in life." Work has become an intrinsic feature of our culture; everyone is now seen as either "deserving" or "undeserving," categories that relate almost entirely to an individual's possession of paid employment or the lack of it (i.e., whether or not they have a job). As Marx so clearly noted in his writings, the owners of the means of production rely on the creation of environments in which work becomes linked to worth. The existence of inherited wealth and the upper middle class (or elite) are still fundamental features of our modern society, but over the last hundred years, in particular, we have increasingly witnessed the merging of aspiration with capitalism, which in turn has solidified liberal ideologies. In order for capitalism to survive and continue to serve a minority group (although this is something we grapple with in chapters 3 and 6), an ideology needs to cement its power over our culture. Reliance on a combination of free market politics and individual choice (agency), makes space for the embedding of capitalism in all aspects of our lives. As Joy White notes, "neo-liberalism masquerades as common sense, inviting us to believe that only the market can deliver goods and services" and that we must all comply with its logic.[28] At the heart of this political and ideological formation is an ableist culture which judges us all to have begun from the same position, and thus to have equal opportunities to adequately contribute to the requirements of capitalist culture. Fundamentally, capitalism, and in turn the project of liberalism, still relies on the marginality of some groups and individuals. The promise it holds out—that it is a way to make life more liveable—is quite clearly embedded in structures of race, class, and gender. For the purpose of an analysis that takes disability seriously, we can see just how the economic subjugation of certain groups becomes a way of justifying our culture. Capitalism relies on the subversion of class consciousness, reproducing an antagonism that asserts that some people are simply more deserving of liveable conditions than others.

Where does neurodiversity fit into this abstract discussion of the perils of capitalism and liberalism? We see that although there are clearly some who are more likely to benefit from these cultures, in essence there are no obvious winners. Ultimately, we see the way our society is currently organized as reproducing loveless cultures, in which even those who can use its resources to manage their lives will seldom experience an entirely healthy existence. As mentioned in the introduction, the potential exists for all people's lives and lifestyles to be changed in an instant by disability. What is required is a recognition that those already grappling with ableist culture need care and love; *those people are us, as well as people we could*—at any moment—*become.*

A Case Study: Workers on the Front Line

Commuting from London to our places of work outside the city means that we regularly witness the local and global consequences of class inequality and the hoarding of wealth and resources. To our right is a city grounded in capitalist culture, fuelled by the global financial markets, the ongoing technological revolution, and the will and ideologies of a continuously evolving bourgeois class. To our left, we see a high proliferation of homeless people on nearly every street. While it is clear that a visible demonstration of inequality can expose the supposed winners as well as the left-behind of capitalist culture, we find that service worker roles clearly demonstrate the possibilities for imagining a more equitable society and recognizing how these matters map on to the effects of neurotypical hegemony. Those who are more likely to be engaging with the sharper ends of material and socially felt inequality are those working in supermarkets, restaurants, and cafes, as well as on trains and buses. These are the people who facilitate our commute to work, and they work in the occupations that kept everybody's lives moving while we lived through the global COVID-19 pandemic and its consequent lockdowns. Of course, these groups also included doctors, nurses, teachers, and other people in the professions designed to look out for us. But the reason we cite here the people who facilitate our commute—a particular sub-section of "service workers," who during the pandemic became commonly known in Britain as *key workers*—is that they show us a clear example of people most often at the forefront of managing and negotiating the consequences of neurotypical hegemony and its capitalist manifestations.

The consequences of neurotypical hegemony, in this instance, are that we have created a society that is largely unsafe for neurodivergent people on a psychological as well as practical basis. This proximity to safety is of course mitigated by our capacity to access resources that make life more liveable. But by and large, those faced with the transgressions of neurotypical culture are the people employed in underpaid service roles who are expected to accept the structural and interpersonal defects it preserves. If an autistic person with a complex relationship to space, people, and transport finds themselves in a mental health "shutdown" in a train station, the first point of call, after other members of the public, will be retail and transport workers. In this moment of shutdown, the autistic person relies on the goodwill of strangers and the capacity of those working in the service industries that surround them to be able to treat them as a human being in need of care, rather than calling the police (and thus making harm much more of an inevitability). On the flip side, the service workers who witness such an event bring to the situation their own class status and position in modern society. We are in no way stating here that working class people are unable to show care to someone in a vulnerable position. We do claim, however, that capitalist culture generates a situation in which this group of workers has to deal, disproportionately, with the impact of a culture that continually marginalizes neurological and mental well-being. Not only are service workers on the front line of negotiating neurotypical hegemony, they also bring to their work and lives a subjectivity informed by the fact that they are underpaid, undervalued, and under-resourced. This group of workers is expected to be empathetic and understanding of neurodivergence and disability in a society that systemically undervalues their existence. Some of the lowest paid people in our society are those who are more likely to have to negotiate the everyday processes of marginalization informed by ableism. Of course, these people are in no way immune from perpetrating harms on the public, and vulnerable people reproduce their own traumas with these workers. But the point is that people are operating and living on inequitable terrain yet are expected to be able to show up for other members of society with the tools to be loving, caring, and understanding of difference. Our material conditions have an impact on how we are able to be, not only in relation to those closest to us, but also to those others who are simply strangers in the street. Here, part of our intentional engagement with service workers is about making the point that these are the people on the front line of neurotypical hegemony and the politics of neurodiversity. This is not to negate the work of parents, carers, and teachers, but more to stress the inextricable links between class, employment, and the obligations bestowed by neurotypical hegemony upon people who are already under material and social pressure.

Up to this point in the book, among other things, we hope to have demonstrated that money and resources are the stepping-stones to dismantling neurotypical hegemony. But in the case of front-line workers, it is clear that class inequality is directly linked to love and care for some of the most vulnerable members of society. This case study is an example of how harm becomes socially reproduced as a result of structures that affect our ability to access ordinary and dignified lives. But it is in such examples that we rely on our more adaptable and able-bodied neurodivergent siblings to recognize that our disabilities are intrinsically linked to our access to capital. In the above example—where the autistic person experiencing shutdown is in a train station—many of us have directly similar experiences or empathy for how this situation can transpire. If such a situation were to escalate, the police would be called and incarceration becomes more likely. We can see that an already stretched workforce is the only point of hope at this moment. Workers on the front line of neurodiversity can be the difference between life and death, dignity or incarceration. With such vignettes, we wish to make clear that to analyze ableism without paying close attention to class and resources limits the possibilities of an emancipatory politics for everyone.

Conclusion

Throughout this chapter we have consistently shown that the analysis of race and class is integral to the work of both exposing and dismantling neurotypical hegemony. While we see this analysis as offering a politics that is both multiclassed and multiethnic, it has been important for us to emphasize that neurodivergence does not—on its own—equate to a socially or materially marginalized life. On the contrary, we have shown that some aspects of neurodivergence lend themselves to our capitalist culture and means of production. In this way, we wanted to make clear that our lived experiences of neurodivergence can sometimes do the work of thwarting emancipatory futures, since the politics of neurodiversity can at times be used as a tool to reproduce individualism and neurotypical hegemony. The middle class and well-resourced neurodivergent individual or population can add to myths around our "superhuman capabilities," or, in more challenging circumstances, about which groups of people, or individuals, may be deserving or undeserving.

There are many within the disability rights and crip theory worlds who have made clear the connections between capitalism and ableism.[29] The instructive nature of this work has been helpful for us as we look back on our childhoods and adult lives so far and recognize just how much of our lived experience has been imbued with a combination of racism, ableism, and capitalism. As we described in chapter 1, there is something about experiencing limited access to resources that stays with you regardless of your acquired class status. In terms of care, and how we see ourselves in society, there is a need to pay attention to the intimate involvement of the state in the process of allocating the resources we—and all neurodivergent people—need. Our postcodes—or simply where we live—remain key factors in the distribution of resources.

Capitalism has always been a reliable barometer of the prevalence of inequity in society, often feeding those who are significantly advantaged and privileged, while simultaneously disadvantaging further those whose lives are more precarious. Social reproduction continues to be a useful mechanism for sustaining a normative—but also exclusionary and decisive—neurotypical hegemony. The arc of capitalism ensures that those who have least access to varying types of social, cultural, and economic capital are more profoundly disadvantaged, resulting in further exacerbation of their neurodivergence. Understanding the plights faced by neurominorities and those with disabilities is important, particularly given the global economic turbulence of the last two decades. Our collective mantra aligns with the need for the democratization and more equitable distribution of societal resources, particularly to neurodivergent families, who struggle—understandably—with uncertainty about how their children, siblings, friends, or relatives are to navigate such exclusionary and unaccommodating spaces. The need to displace capitalism from our society in favor of more emancipatory and equitable structures is central to the creation of a culture that provides better outcomes for the neurodivergent community. One part of such displacement involves accepting that society is unequal and that this inequality straddles all our major institutions. Class mobility gives you the power to challenge experts. We can only truly engage with the social model if such engagement involves routes to economic equity. This is of course both racialized and classed. A Black mother from a working-class background must deal with multiple objections to her parenting and decision-making, and the reason why all classes should care about this is that we all live in the same society. We will never change our views on neurodiversity if only the middle and upper class are supported and successful.

Neurotypical hegemony thrives on structural inequality. All-pervading inequality is sustained by the well-oiled stratification of society. Given the resources invested in maintaining and sharpening such instruments, the challenge is how we might collectively pierce, and so disrupt, this omnipresent neurotypical hegemony, which requires the displacement of that which society has cemented as normal. Allies of neurodivergence and disability rights have often trodden the thorny path of greater equality for all, and while significant gains have been made, the ability of these normative instruments to reinvent themselves means that they continue to exist. The persistence of this societal marginalization hampers the possibilities for a more tolerant society that embraces neurodivergent people.

6

Everything Is Everything

MERITOCRACY, ELITISM, AND HOW WE CREATE VALUE

It seems we lose the game
Before we even start to play
Who made these rules?
We're so confused

(LAURYN HILL, 1998)

FROM LEARNING to talk at the age of eleven to speaking to millions of people on TV as a thirty-nine-year-old man, song lyrics have always been central to how Jason makes sense of society and the relationships we create within it. Whether he is talking to teachers about leadership or helping students to apply theory to practice in their sociology essays, there is a song for everything. As music helped us to piece together the chapter themes of the book, we would certainly encourage all readers to think about how different arts or forms of creative expression can guide us when seeking to explain and even come to terms with our very existence as human beings. Music has been an essential component of our methodology, especially when it comes to introducing the more abstract aspects of our discussions. Further, each page was inspired by the sounds, lyrics, and arrangements of songs that have guided us in our quest to make neurodivergent scholarship a more normal practice in academia. We return to these types of more holistic reflections to help us introduce this chapter on (the myth of) meritocracy, elitism, and value. We see neurodivergent scholarship as integral to a future where theories about life and society can be more inclusive and better suited for practical application.

This chapter is—like all the others—musically framed, and this time we were inspired by the conscious hip-hop lyrics of the generation-defining Lauryn Hill. As we began to think about how to discuss themes related to meritocracy, value, and elitism, her song, "Everything Is Everything," a track from the groundbreaking album, *The Miseducation of Lauryn Hill*, felt like an obvious choice.[1] This song was especially significant for us in this chapter, as it helps to connect some of our biggest challenges for the creation of the loving frameworks and language that will best *take people with us*. Part of the beautiful yet challenging aspects of Hill's narrative in "Everything Is Everything" is the recognition that *life is and it isn't* but also that we are deserving of fulfilment, love, and happiness regardless of the ups and downs of everyday life. In this way, some of the arguments we have proposed and contribute to in this book require a complete rethink of how we understand each other. We recognize that this kind of reconsideration of society requires a combination of creativity and real-life examples of what this will look like in practice. In short, it is not a given that people will have an equitable chance of an ordinary and dignified life, despite the promotion of the message, throughout civil society, that this is the case for everyone regardless of their background.

Returning to the track for this chapter, "Everything Is Everything" is a song that contains lyrics that relate to a Black diasporic sense of "realness," empowerment, and struggle. Hill's lyrics are a poetic instruction to young people to accept the inevitability of struggle in our formative years, which also recognize the value of commitment to self-love and seeking to assert or reassure them that *"change will come eventually."* The lyrics—*"It seems we lose the game, before we even start to play / let's love ourselves and we can't fail / to make a better situation / tomorrow, our seeds will grow / all we need is dedication"*—give a near perfect summary of how we plan to explore the myth of meritocracy, value, and elitism in this chapter. Bear with us, as we broach some big debates in this discussion—we are confident that it is through discussions about what is—and which groups of people or individuals are—considered valuable, that we can truly begin to dismantle neurotypical hegemony.

Setting the Scene

The chapter explores how the social reproduction of the myth of meritocracy, elitism, and value produces a convergence of cultures and beliefs in relation to work, education, and our capacity to achieve an ordinary and dignified social life. We draw on the themes addressed throughout the book to build a theoretical and practical presentation of how modern neoliberal society creates the terrain for neurodiversity to become commodified, which in turn becomes a mechanism to maintain the cultures and beliefs we explore in this discussion. Naming these processes is not only an essential part of demonstrating how neurotypical hegemony is maintained, however, but also crucially provides us with some discursive routes into its dismantling.

Critical engagement with the myths of meritocracy, elitism, and value is essential for the deconstruction of neurotypical hegemony. The arguments in this chapter build on the discussions in chapters 4 and 5 by understanding that the concept of value, in particular, has developed in a way that consistently thwarts our potential to build emancipatory dialects in the politics of neurodiversity. The question of what sorts of people or individuals are considered to be of value creates cultures in which "worth," "productivity," and "authenticity" become synonymous with neurotypical hegemony. Closer proximity to the neuromajority is a route into a social life in which the rules are simply laid out. Read, listen, and control your emotions and eventually become a member of civil society; someone who is not only "civil" but also productive. In a way similar to our own reminders about which groups of people are able to access an ordinary and dignified life, Chapman and Carel have suggested that medical model approaches to autism specifically generate dialogues that pathologize autists in ways that deem them unable to access "the good life." They note that the good life has become a societal conception of what it means to flourish as both child and adult and that a neurodiversity paradigm (which shifts how we understand neurological functioning), and specifically the politics of neurodiversity, is conceived as being at odds with the idea of the "good" and the "normal."[2] For us, this notion of the good life amounts to a representation of what and who becomes valued, since we know that the neurotypical majority is not simply made up of those who have garnered valuable status in social life through their ability to tick the greatest number of neurologically acceptable boxes. As with all the themes we have laid out throughout the book, other aspects of social life like family, work, and education provide useful prompts for showing rather than telling how neurotypical domination obstructs routes to love and acceptance through its creation of notions of value that are detrimental to any society seeking to create an equitable culture.

As with the arguments we make in other chapters, we have intentionally drawn on our own Black and neurodivergent subjectivity in this chapter to provide a framework through which to view the social production of value through race, class, and disability. Further, our conceptualization of what constitutes an ordinary and good life is supplemented by the work of other scholars of inequality. Put simply, other forms of structural marginalization can also help to demonstrate how value becomes normalized. Our own lived experience has been inserted as a starting point for analysis to produce an instructive discourse that aligns with a variety of other experiences. As Black educators inspired by our siblings' activism and scholarship, but also by the philosophies of Aristotle, we are reminded that at the heart of what we do is the discussion and imagination of a world which takes seriously the fusion of the universal (how we take everyone with us) and the particular (how we stress that we all start from different places, spaces, and structures of society in our attempts to achieve a dignified life). Put simply, abandoning value, elitism, and meritocracy will eventually be emancipatory even for the groups who have materially benefitted so much more from the inequitable structures of society.

The myth of meritocracy and elitism rely on one another. Crucially, they facilitate the grounds and politics of value. Embedded in much of our discussion in this book has been an ongoing acknowledgement that value is something acquired, which is directly linked to the ongoing maintenance of neurotypical hegemony. For the purpose of this chapter, we recognize that the notions of "hard work," "achievement," and "success" are things that grant individuals space, either closer to, or inside, the elite. In turn, we can show that in the space where power creates opportunity, those inhabiting the higher end of the structure are seen as the most valuable. Crucially, as the most valuable, they are also positioned as those who most deserve this valued status. As Bev Skeggs notes, to be valued is to be granted the status that affirms that you are worthy and *you are proper.*[3]

Across society, neurotypical culture makes clear that those who can adhere to its ways and constraints are more likely to be positioned as valued and deserving of love. This culture positions love as dignity and ordinariness, but also as the chance to make mistakes. This is what is so crucial about the notion of being valued. It isn't that you are just expected to *always get it right.* To be valued means you are allowed to make mistakes, fall off the horse and get back on. To experience value is to know that you are seen as productive enough to be worthy of the ups and downs of everyday life. Value is what is given to lives and people seen as contributing to society in a way that maintains the circulation of its shared beliefs. As we began to introduce in chapter 5, these matters are intrinsically linked to the historical and contemporary formations of capitalism. We recognize here that value can be acquired (often tentatively) if you have been deemed a worthy participant in the means of production.

Public Debate and Value

During the summer of writing this book we spent much of our time watching the news. As we introduced in chapter 1, we are writing at a time where poverty and disparities in wealth are at unprecedented levels. In particular, we know that children and single people in Britain, as well as disabled people and the elderly, are facing some of the toughest daily challenges when it comes to food poverty and the ability to heat their homes. Over the past ten years, people receiving social security benefits have not had their level of financial assistance increased in line with earnings or inflation.[4] The disabled community is among these groups and contains families who are struggling to participate in capitalist and ableist culture. Further, we are seeing increasing pressure on, and cuts in the funding of, special educational needs (SEN) schools and many teachers and social workers now contend that these institutions are at breaking point. Here we return to schools and education as a way of introducing the social reproduction of value by a variety of factors that rely on existing class antagonisms. A news item published on the BBC News website in May 2023 cited a debate on the Educational Health and Care Plan (EHCP) initiatives of Kent County Council, which featured comments from the Conservative Councillor for Maidstone, Simon Webb, about the parents applying for this.[5] "Where are the gatekeepers?" he said. "If I am a parent who thinks that their child needs an EHCP,[6] because that's the in thing to do as a parent these days, who is going to turn around and say no?" He said that parents see, "all the add-ons that go with it and they think, 'This is bloody good. Let's go for it.'"

In a very similar set of circumstances in January 2024, a video clip on the BBC News website of Conservative councillors in Warwickshire debating the reasons for an increase in spending on Special Educational Needs and Disabilities (SEND) support for children in the local area, provoked the anger of parents when Councillor Brian Hammersley asked: "Does anyone know why this is increasing so rapidly? Is it something in the water? Why are there so many people now jumping out with these needs? Where were they in the past when I was at school? I never heard of SEND [at that time]."[7]

Another Councillor, Jeff Morgan, commenting on the need to restrain spending, said: "I don't know how you do that apart from being tougher, asking more penetrating questions, not automatically accepting the plea of a mother saying that little

Willy has ADHD when in actual fact little Willy is just really badly behaved and needs some form of strict correction."

These comments contain a set of ideologies that are becoming more and more socially acceptable among both public officials and the general public. Here we return to schools as a way of showing just how strongly neurotypical hegemony is able to reproduce itself. The comments above, made by sitting councillors in Britain, demonstrate a lack of care and understanding of disability, while also putting forward arguments related to "trends," discipline, and "gatekeeping." We use these quotes from councillors to begin to introduce how our engagement with the idea of value in relation to the ways neurotypical hegemony is upheld has been guided by the re-emergence of public debates on the matter of disability and the politics of neurodiversity. Questions surrounding the issue of who is of value and who deserves to have their needs met have reached the point where children and families are being exposed to levels of scrutiny that are often devoid of lived experience and embedded in individual agency and class antagonisms. There are those who seek to question the value of people's concern about the distribution of resources out of (what they consider to be) moral objections. Crucially, however, there are also those who seek to use language and discourse like that of the councillors cited above to acquire capital and further embed cultures of neurotypical hegemony.

In our regular conversations about how disability is discussed in public spheres, we often returned to the pundits, journalists, and "intellectuals" who seemed to be "brand building" on the grounds that those who are marginalized invariably contained groups of ungrateful and ungracious people. Many people understand marginality and inequality to be matters of individual choice. And watching these well-rehearsed discourses on "scroungers" and undeserving groups take on new forms,[8] we observe the resurgence of some exceptionally antagonistic public debates that seem to be reaching particularly pernicious levels. We see these cultures as crucial to the backlash against the Black Lives Matter movement of 2016 and 2020 and the eugenicist choices and cultures upheld by governments since the COVID-19 global pandemic. Voices fixated on creating values that disregard race, class, gender, and disability have become a way to contribute to the ideological state apparatus, as well as simply a renewed way of making money. In respect of the arguments in this chapter, we see this process as grounded in questions about *who is valued* and the ways in which media and governments use public and policy platforms to embed such ideas into the ways we live and relate to each other. These questions of value are an extension of our arguments about capitalism in chapter 4.

There is money to be made in creating content that questions whether Black or disabled life is of value. Those who create such content see our conversations about racism and ableism as futile, denying an existence in which structures, rather than "hard work," determine outcomes. With an empathetic eye, and in our attempt to find common ground, something we both observe in these people is a mistrust of the very system they seem to be upholding, as well as a general sense of unhappiness. Other critical scholars might see what we are trying to do here as a red herring—a critique that we both understand and appreciate. But for us the constant message is about the deserving and the undeserving, and about the fact that even those who benefit both structurally and materially from the idea that meritocracy exists seem to be dissatisfied. As Robbie Shilliam has noted, the operationalizing of outrage, mistrust, and blame becomes a by-product of postcolonial societies seeking to mobilize notions of deserving- and undeserving-ness as a means to divide and rule multiethnic working-class populations and further maintain hierarchies of power.[9] We seek to intervene here by emphasizing the uses and possibilities of the politics of neurodiversity as a unifying mechanism that can help destroy myths around people, value, and deservingness. Part of our work is to discuss disability and neurodiversity in a more universal way; it is also about speaking to the people who see the system as equitable simply by virtue of its existence. It is not that we are convinced that we can change people's minds, but that we see the value in making clear to everyone exactly what it is we are upholding and defending, because a lot of the hope we draw on throughout this book comes from the idea that—by making its means of operation transparent—we can show people a system that they might want to question and maybe help to dismantle. With the talking heads who take pleasure in denying the existence of racism and ableism, it might be that one of the few ways we can actually get them to understand is by breaking down the various ways that the current system is causing them angst. We are not naïve in our assessments of the far right here; we are aware that there is money to be made, not just in denying our struggles but also in denying our very existence. But there is a part of us that almost obsesses over the idea that there is always humanity to be retrieved from what often feels like *the road to nowhere*. The only way to truly dismantle the myth of meritocracy is to change the way people respond to or receive the idea that hard work automatically secures a positive and secure sense of self.

As we laid out in chapter 1, most people are in closer proximity to neurodiversity than they would probably like to believe or admit. A trend that we have seen across society is that people tend to understand marginality through direct experience or the experience of someone close to them. Critical scholars trying to imagine more equitable futures might be better off conceding that one of the only ways we are going to be able to get a more universal understanding of inclusion is by recognizing that some people can only really have that light bulb moment when they are physically and emotionally close to the matters we are discussing in this book. This might be a concession that helps support the building of future bridges of familiarity through difference. Perhaps it would make a difference if we could convince those people, who were once at odds with our perspectives but who have come to understand our arguments, to speak to the groups in which they used to be intellectually housed.

One of the Black British feminist practitioners, teachers and activists whose work we draw on here is Stella Dadzie, best known for being a founding member of the Organization of Women of African and Asian Descent (OWAAD) in the 1970s, and co-authoring—with Suzanne Scafe and Beverley Bryan—the book *The Heart of the Race: Black Women's Lives in Britain* (1985). In 1997, Dadzie published a report titled *Blood, Sweat and Tears: A Report of the Bede Anti-Racist Detached Youth Work Project* based on a youth work project she had led that was dedicated to combatting racism in a community in London. Based on the evidence of racism targeted at Black people in a London borough, the project focused on the perpetrators of racist activity, and on providing anti-racist education for the local white community as a way of combatting the frustrations and political impotence of the mainly white and working-class young people.[10] It is this kind of work that has very much inspired both of our trajectories. We stand on the shoulders of Black feminists like Dadzie, who herself is part of a long history of radical educationalists, in acknowledging that part of an intentional recognition of the structures of our current society involves working humbly in service of a vision of the society we would like to belong to.

In addition to the inspirational work of Black feminist activists, we also recognize here that as neurodivergent people we can become experts in the different ways that value is assigned, simply by being, very often, outside neurotypical ways of being. As with the white youth Dadzie sought to educate, who acted out their misdirected class frustrations on their Black peers, we see neurodivergent people as having an exceptionally intimate understanding of the convergence of value and class. We have learnt that we can often only acquire truly valued status if our "exceptional capabilities" align with capitalist modalities. For example, if our neurodivergence can add value by being faster, more profitable, or (what has been deemed) more efficient, it then becomes something to appreciate. Our lives are like a long distance run in which the idea—and the status!—of the valued subject is at the end or finish line. The problem for us is that someone (or society itself) keeps moving the finish line. It is clear how easily this can be applied to those at the sharper ends of classed and racialized inequity. The powers of endurance required to deal with this effect of neurodivergence at the same time as dealing with the effects of race and other intersecting variables (such as sexism and classism), affect our physical and mental health (see chapter 3). This is why a critical understanding of value is so important for disability justice and all social justice work. The consequences of value can be deadly, and much of what we want to discuss, in relation to value and elitism, involves stressing that the parameters of the ideal human, as this is defined in our culture, maligns a lot of society. The vision we have, as neurodivergent scholars, comes from our ability to bear witness to the sharper ends of this maligning and to highlight how value has become a slippery, invisible, yet omnipresent aspect of contemporary society. In an effort to challenge and eventually erase them, we can identify these processes by shining a light on the idea of value in all aspects of social life.

Parts of this book have been uncomfortable to write, simply because so many of us are socialized to believe that the way society is organized—in spite of systemic inequality—still provides a route to a dignified life, well endowed with resources and (of course) loving. What is even more uncomfortable is that the harms that keep these structures in place also rely on the perspectives and actions of people we love and respect. The intimacy in which hegemony—and in the case of this book, neurotypical hegemony—operates is a matter for us to name, explore, and challenge if we are to truly eradicate it. In this way, our friends, community, and disabled siblings are all socially conditioned to reproduce the cultures of consent that decide who is considered the most valuable citizen. These uncomfortable realities do, however, do the work of recognizing that inequality, marginality, and specifically neurotypical hegemony cannot be explained by the notions of "good" and "bad people." In many cases, the existence of power—and its dynamics—limits the possibility that we can truly dismantle neurotypical hegemony. Paying attention to the intimate and routine nature of our proximity to cultures harmful to neurodiversity does actually provide us with routes to get out. And who better to convince about ideological control than those who love and are in community with us? In the simplest sense, we began these reflections on our own subjective engagements with value, meritocracy, and elitism with the honest reflection that we are all susceptible to reproducing culture, and this reality, in itself, tells us exactly what we are up against when it comes to neurotypical hegemony.

When we came to think practically about how to dismantle neurotypical hegemony, we realized that many of the examples on which we have drawn in this book consider the importance of work. As academics based at Oxford and Cambridge, we have attempted to bridge the fact that we have experienced the perils of racism and ableism intensely yet have still managed to end up at two of the most well-resourced institutions in the world. While we still see possibility in our own reflections on marginality at work, we understand that we are the lucky ones and that to both reflexively and humbly discuss marginalization we have to keep in mind that we are by now firmly middle-class academics, even if we have not lost our ability to see the many experiences in our careers to date that demonstrate how value, meritocracy, and elitism become racialized, as well as how this process is itself reliant on ableism. As we have claimed throughout the book, the way that racism is produced in conjunction with ableism and capitalism is a central aspect of neurotypical hegemony.

Why (the Myth of) Meritocracy Matters

One of our core themes relates to the fact that how we navigate life, particularly in our earlier years on the planet, is very much informed by where we sit in the social structure. Class, race, ethnicity, gender, and nation are just some of the key social reproductions that can have a demonstrable impact on our routes through life. We want to be sure, in our critique of meritocracy, that we also acknowledge people's agency and the fact that many are not constrained by the circumstances into which they are born. Nonetheless, we still see a return to the idea that our society is a meritocracy as an essential component of dismantling neurotypical power.

Throughout the book we have sought to demonstrate the varying ways that neurotypical hegemony obstructs a neurodivergent person's sense of self, as well as how this culture is harmful even for the neuromajority. Across education and the workplace, the categories that are considered normal and reasonable are "decided" by neurotypical hegemony. These socially constructed ideas determine how society should be organized and have come to be aligned with notions of harmony and cohesion. To question the cultures of neurotypical hegemony is synonymous with being unruly or seeking to cause disorder. Yet the social parameters of cohesion, determined by the notion of meritocracy, do not serve the vast majority of people. While we recognize the wider mechanisms that may advance the prevailing narrative that meritocracy serves society well, it is also important to note that such narratives are in direct opposition to a harmonious society that embraces difference.

The idea of a meritocratic society is one that suggests that anyone with the ability can succeed regardless of their background. All they have to do is try their best and social mobility is a guaranteed outcome. The myth of meritocracy is that success is a marker of both ability and hard work or rather, that if you are not successful it is because you were not clever enough or did not work hard enough. Meritocratic principles put social failings like poverty, poor education, and ill-health back on to the individual, who is seen to lack the ability and work ethic to improve their circumstances.

Michael Young is often claimed to have coined the term "meritocracy," in his 1958 satirical discussion, *The Rise of the Meritocracy*.[11] He wrote about a fictional society in which ability plus hard work guaranteed achievement, social status, and reward. The fictional society was used by Young to address how the inequality produced by meritocratic principles leads people in the lower classes to embody the belief that failure is an individual (rather than structural) matter. Young's essay is satirical because in reality the elite, the wealthy and powerful are much more likely to inherit their wealth and therefore much more easily acquire their "valued" status simply by virtue of not being in poverty and therefore able to purchase social goods like education and health. For those of us who are not in proximity to the groups that can give one a "leg up," so to speak, the idea is that working hard produces the terrain for meritocracy to flourish in any walk of life. According to Ansgar Allen, the key point that Young was trying to make was that an immense amount of trust is bound up in civil society and its institutions to govern, teach, and guide all citizens to reach their full potential.[12]

The fact that we are writing this from our positions in the ivory tower of academia could be used to refute our arguments and assert that meritocracy exists. We have each experienced a version of academic success that allows us to be seen as the "valued" neurodivergent person. We can see how our career trajectories could be held up as evidence that the meritocracy exists (equality of opportunity) and that it works for everyone (even people with all the disadvantages we have can still achieve). After Jason was appointed the youngest ever Black professor at University of Cambridge in 2023, the global media was captivated by his story of learning to speak at the age of eleven, and to read and write at eighteen. We often saw the subtext of the publicity surrounding Jason's professorship as insinuating: "if he can do it, then so can anyone." This type of subtext ignores the truth, that not everyone can have the "top" positions in society even if only because there are not enough of them to go around. What we need to make clear is that the system of value we seek to unpack here is flexible enough to allow some people from the so-called lower classes (or Black or neurodivergent people) to succeed, something that can be turned against those who do not.

For us as sociologists, it feels surreal that we still have to make the case that meritocracy is a myth in 2024. This particular myth has endured and flourished through capitalistic endeavor. While we recognize the various ways in which society reproduces the idea that intellect plus hard work leads to upward social mobility, we see no reason for this myth to persist. At the very least, such myths require active disruption to establish a discourse that recognizes that what is called meritocracy is actually (in the main) privilege for the few and not the overwhelming majority. When considering the relationship between neurodiversity and meritocracy, it is important to note that in many instances, an absolute belief in meritocracy can determine whether a neurodivergent person is received and treated as a human being. It can be the difference between life and death, love or disposability. This notion of "merit" has historically failed to consider the discriminatory factors that compromise individuals' ability to access this most crystallized of societal norms.

All this being said, as critical scholars we also have a duty to recognize that the social reproduction of meritocracy is substantially supported by the perceived cultural turn that involves a democratization of resources and information about life, education, and work. The digital and technological revolution has in many ways increased access, but what we need to come to terms with is that the idea that everything is accessible has also meant that we have taken our collective foot off the gas when it comes to making clear that meritocracy has always been a myth.

From Meritocracy to Elitism

At various points in this book we have discussed the connected social reproductions of racism, ableism and capitalism. We use this language to refer to people and cultures pivotal to the protection and production of inequality and thus of neurotypical hegemony. We believe that no one is born with the desire to be a part of a group or society that uses the marginalization of others to keep their social and economic standing and safety in society. But we do see a combination of conscious awareness and learned ignorance about the existence of a class structure as something with which the elite are comfortable. We define the elite as people whose earnings are in the top one percent, those who govern and lead countries, and those with ownership and control of the global media. In the more traditional sense, they are the people in the royal domain, as well as the families who make money through the sale of the goods and services that we see as essential to our functionality. They are also the highest earners in the tech and pharma industries. The elite come from a range of places, spaces, and walks of life and are continually winning across multiple fronts. We consent to the elite controlling the fundamental features of everyday life.

At the heart of this chapter is our rallying call for a renewed acknowledgement of the realities of the myth of meritocracy as an integral part of the dismantling of neurotypical hegemony. We see more recent cultures across the worlds of work, education, and social life—and even amongst our fellow sociologists— as neglecting the fact that "intellect, ability, and hard work" do not inevitably grant a peaceful, dignified, and fulfilled existence in civil society. These myths rely on the existence of a stratified and intensely felt class culture that produces both the elite and the elite(ism) that sustains it (see chapter 5). In the majority of the humanist and Black feminist analysis found throughout this book, the crucial aspect of the myth of meritocracy and the inevitable protection it grants to elites and elitism is that it is consented to across civil society. In its core suggestion that those who experience marginalization could make different choices that would help them to access (or become part of) the elite we can see how the idea of meritocracy provides the basis for elitism to flourish. Our concern in this more abstract chapter about how we end up socially producing the most valuable citizen is that all these considerations rely on a multiclassed and multiethnic acceptance of the way things are. This acceptance of (or consent to) the way things are is exactly how hegemony works; simply put, the protection of the elite is grounded in civil society.

The notion of meritocracy has inadvertently created a club of people convinced of the straightforward nature of success and achievement in life. The challenging aspect of this reality was covered in chapter 5, where we made clear that early and even life-long experiences of material and socioeconomic struggle are no guarantee that a person will end up in possession of a critical view of the structural and inevitable nature of inequality. As we put forward the case, deep into the first quarter of the twenty-first century, that meritocracy is a myth, we oppose the proposition by those who have had a very similar lived experience of class, race, and disability, that none of these issues can stop an individual gaining an education, safe employment, and fulfilling relationships. Loyalty to the myth that meritocracy is alive and well provides routes into the cultures and conversations that protect elitism. Rahman Khan notes that the study of elites and elitism is the study of power and inequality.[13] But it is at this juncture between meritocracy and elitism that we find not only the social reproduction of value (see later in this chapter) but also the unique vista provided by the notion of neurotypical hegemony that has brought us to this point in the analysis. The normalization of meritocracy relies on the consent of groups who are in no way guaranteed membership of, or access to, the benefits that elitism provides. Broadly speaking, the aspirational nature of the capitalist condition (see chapter 2) creates fertile terrain for the social reproduction of the myth of meritocracy by the very people it seeks to marginalize, blame, and victimize. Taking a brief detour to the neurodivergent individual, when we speak to some of our siblings we are always surprised at the directions these conversations can take when we discuss the social and economic steps required to access an ordinary and dignified life. The myth of meritocracy creates a culture that confirms many of the fears current among neurodivergent communities—fears about themselves and their place in society. Social conditioning as well as our neurological status means we become disproportionately susceptible to self-deprecation, blame, and in more troubling scenarios, a more internalized and continuous criticism of our sense of self in general (see chapter 3). The connection here is twofold. At the intersection of neurodiversity and class, first of all, we can see how those who are able to mobilize their agency to alter their structural position exemplify the proposition, essential to the idea of meritocracy, that inequality is not determined. But this in turn produces the discourse that neurodiversity can either help people access opportunities in a meritocracy, or that it is something that people negotiate but which does not create a determined outcome. The reality of this analysis is that both of these can be true. Our concern is the existence of these truths outside a more standardized, empathetic, and realistic representation of the lives of the most structurally marginalized. Love and care is needed as people find their way through this society, which calls for both a material and an ideological evolution of how we approach all people. The revival of a true cultural and practical dismantling of the myth of meritocracy runs alongside the dismantling of neurotypical hegemony.

These matters become particularly challenging and at times troubling on a more interpersonal basis because we are dealing with the tension between structure and agency. It is these tensions that we lean into and resist (see chapter 2). This provides routes to addressing the way that neurotypical hegemony relies on the personal, political, and structural. We need to emphasize the power, not only of structure but also of individual agency to make the changes we need to truly dismantle neurotypical hegemony. The two groups for whom the challenge of naming and eradicating neurotypical hegemony matters most are those who are guaranteed entry to the elite and those who are marginalized by the myth of meritocracy, yet still feel that if they possessed the right (innate) personal qualities, that they would be able to succeed and ultimately—be seen as valuable (see next section). Our analysis is not limited to this dualistic interpretation, although acknowledging the existence of both groups when it comes to the combination of meritocracy and elitism identifies the difficulty of the challenge at hand. But membership of either of these groups is not guaranteed; by their very nature they are socially constructed and can be unmade. And it is in the middle ground here, or among those who have a foot in each camp, that much of the power to deconstruct the myth of meritocracy resides. Their power is in the fact that they can create spaces within their lives that intentionally recognize the existence of a stratified culture that keeps the cycle of inequality in motion. They are our families, our friends, our co-workers, our leaders, and the strangers who walk past us in the street. In fact, they are all of us. As we return to our two hypothetical groups, we want to stress again that instead of mindlessly socially reproducing this culture of meritocracy we can choose to play a part in resisting the elite and their values while at the same time advocating for the lives of the marginalized. Power too often remains unnamed and unchecked and we know that in our social lives there are moments, conversations, and decisions in which—if we choose to act one way rather than another—we can counter its dominance.

The primary issue created by a belief in meritocracy is the entrenchment of elitism; that is, the social reproduction of the concentration of power and status among a small but highly influential group of elites. What we see as a delicate, yet high relatable connection between meritocracy and elitism is crucial to the protection of structures of neurotypical domination. While the notion of meritocracy continues to shape the access people are given to live ordinary and dignified lives, we continue to accept a culture in which a select few are able to mitigate issues of social mobility through the existence of networks and capital. It is clear that this interplay between a belief in meritocracy and the existence of elitism can also be beneficial for some neurodivergent individuals who have proximity to (economic, cultural, and social) capital, which can help suppress the perils of neurotypical hegemony. This demonstrates the importance of moving beyond an individualized understanding of neurodiversity and neurotypical hegemony, since proximity to or membership of the elite can thwart the subjective consciousness of those it seeks to marginalize.

The point we have addressed here is that the grounds on which elitism is built are created when only some individuals have access to certain opportunities and are rewarded on the basis of their supposed "merit," leading members of the elite to believe in the fairness and equality of the system.

From Meritocracy to Elitism to Value

Much of the discussion in this book has focused on the need to dismantle neurotypical hegemony to create routes for all people to access a dignified and ordinary life. We see the emphasis on societal productivity as synonymous with neurotypical culture, and as producing environments that favor the capacity to mask, adapt, and adhere to the ways of the neuromajority. In this chapter, we have so far engaged with the concept of value, while also making clear the connection between this, the myth of meritocracy, and elitism. We see the interplay between these social processes as crucial to the way neurotypical hegemony evolves and adapts in our society, as it continues to win across multiple fronts. Those in power have the most to lose from dismantling this ideology and need the rest of us to keep believing that ability and hard work will pay off. And where there is a gendered and racialized gap in the diagnosis of neurodiversity, or where the provision of reasonable adjustments in school and work rely on the will of the individual, we can see just how crucial it is to expose as false the belief in meritocracy and the type of society it produces. As we link this idea more strongly to the elite and elitism, we begin to see the ways in which a select group of people (usually) takes the lead in protecting neurotypical hegemony.

The combination of meritocracy and elitism has led to a protected system where value is placed on "measurable" achievements and skills. Elitism is sustained by those with proximity to the notion of merit, or who are themselves members of the elite—the most valuable positions across civil society. Elitism is created through a supposedly meritocratic framework that becomes the benchmark of value. But as with all of our discussions throughout this book, we have to make clear the ways that neurodiversity can be co-opted into these cultures and social reproductions. The appearance of including neurodivergent sensibilities does the work of covertly maintaining the cyclical nature of neurotypical dominance and hegemony. Put simply and returning to the other issues raise throughout the book, the interplay between meritocracy, elitism, and value relies on the partial inclusion of some neurodivergent people.

Capitalism and the Commodification of Neurodiversity

Throughout the book so far, one of the key sites of contention has been a growing concern among the neurodivergent community about the commodification of our existence. The discourse that situates our marginality as sets of individual stories routinely positions neurodivergence as something to be overcome. During this process we create hierarchies of struggle that become the blueprint for deciding what and whose story matters more. There are of course many different experiences within the neurodivergent community that clearly need representation, but in present circumstances this involves assigning value to neurodivergence in a way that commodifies our struggle. On the one hand, we position certain neurodivergent stories as representative of the most authentic or valued experience. On the other hand, the neurodiverse community as a whole is not valued because society is based on the premise that neurotypicality produces the most valuable subject. As we continue to grapple with the existence of the double-edged sword of the neo-liberal approach to neurodiversity, there are aspects of the former that—in the present moment—need to be flagged up. More and more we are seeing that the most valued neurodivergent (and disability) story or existence is one that complies with and benefits the means of production (see chapter 4). To be a valued neurodivergent individual in contemporary society means possessing the ability to produce capital in spite of being neurodivergent or disabled or being able to "do things" that neuromajorities cannot.

A general theme during our discussions about the maintenance of neurotypical hegemony in civil society has been the existence of neoliberal economics and ideologies. Promoting deregulation and privatization, as well as a belief in individuals' liberty to succeed, neoliberalism is perhaps the political cornerstone of everything we have discussed in this book. The central tenets of neoliberalism are its emphases on competition and individualism. The idea that these two structural and interpersonally led mechanisms can provide efficiency of course produces a culture neurodivergent individuals can acquire and to which they can conform. Although we have steered clear of describing neurodivergent traits and brains, for the purpose of addressing how the co-option of neurodiversity becomes part of sustaining neurotypical hegemony, it is important to sidestep into the way that representing a simultaneity between neurodiversity and productivity in modern neoliberal society does much to entrench meritocracy, elitism and value.

In chapter 5, we discussed how we are currently at a capitalist conjuncture where both global and local private organizations and institutions are stating that their businesses have a vested interest in the inclusion and progression of neurodivergent people. The emphasis on our divergent perspectives and "innovative" skills has been repackaged as something that makes us worthy of inclusion. Of course, we know that this is a culture that has existed for many years prior to our inclusion in it. But the equality, diversity, and inclusion complex, which has a powerful, global message, has become linked to the way neurodiversity becomes commodified. Of course, some neurodivergent people are already considered to be of value. These people are by and large those who are able to assimilate into neurotypical society through the means of production. The means of production in this sense is composed of a variety of capitals. These capitals relate to financial as well as other more fluid forms of value. This fluidity can be found in the marketability of difference. Difference can be consumed as entertainment, and at any given moment, there are strands of neurodivergence that become associated with this.

Conclusion

In this chapter we have addressed how a combination of meritocracy, elitism, and value is integral to the cultural, ideological, and practical (institutional) creation and maintenance of neurotypical hegemony. We have demonstrated the ongoing interplay between these three social reproductions, with each providing the criteria for the formation of consent and common sense across civil society. We have also demonstrated the intrinsic link between value and neurotypical hegemony, arguing that meritocracy produces elitism which then creates value. This formula relies on the creation of neurotypical hegemony and dominance. Historically speaking, notions of intellectual ability and mental health have been used to stratify populations and used ideologically to condone material inequality and incarceration. In the more everyday sense, notions of intellect and mental illness have produced discourses across a multitude of cultures and belief systems that have designated which groups and individuals deserve an ordinary and dignified existence (see chapter 3). We have attempted here to theorize the way these three concepts not only rely on each other but are also crucial for the protection of neurotypical hegemony. Moreover, we have illustrated throughout the book so far that this is all socially constructed and thus by its very nature can be undone. This is where the possibilities of love and hope can truly be actualized. By following our framework—in which, we acknowledge, we sometimes name the obvious, as well as being transparent about what these unnamed cultures are doing—we can see the possibilities of equitable and emancipatory futures.

It is difficult for us to talk about value and to deconstruct its impact. We are not ashamed to admit that the value of value is something that—even as neurodivergent people—we are at risk of reproducing. This comes back to the (societal) race in which we are ourselves trying to be valued, so to be critical of this process means abandoning what we have aspired to become. This is not to say that we have aspired to be neurotypical, but we have aspired to be valued. Unpacking value in this way probably means removing the word entirely. There is no hierarchy in our utopia and in our re-imagination of society value is replaced by love and care for everyone. Or, simply put, our very existence will be evidence of our value.

7

For Tomorrow

A MANIFESTO FOR DISMANTLING NEUROTYPICAL HEGEMONY

She's a twentieth century girl
Holding on for dear life
And so we hold each other tightly
And hold on for tomorrow

(BLUR, 1993)

THE ESSEX quartet of Albarn, Coxon, James, and Rowntree is enshrined in British folklore as one of the archetypes of Brit-pop, and more famously as the arch-nemesis of their Mancunian rivals Oasis of Burnage (readers should have gathered from the title of this book that this rivalry is not something that affects our love for either band!). Throughout the hedonism of the 1990s, both bands *held one another tightly* and often for dear life. For neurodivergent people, who are often holding on to the coattails of neurotypicals, there is a need for the neuromajority population to be more accommodating and understanding in this process . . . and *hold on for tomorrow.*

As we began to round up our reflections and the rationale of the book, we spoke a lot about the concept of time and our general sense of *getting through the day*. Though we feel as if this is something that is likely to be felt by all people at certain points in their life, disability can often make one feel that each day is a battle. Bringing together the mantras of Blur as well as our own personal provocations, we recount that it is one day at a time, we need to put one foot in front of the other, but that there is always an aspiration for living *for tomorrow*. Whether in our personal or professional lives, we do what we need to do each day to get through neurotypical hegemony and its cultures. But what we would like to make clear in this concluding chapter is that this sense of "surviving" each day could be something we let go of as a society. The parameters we put in place for our families, relationships, work, and education seldom *need* to be organized according to the principles of neurotypical hegemony. It does not have to be inevitable that a whole swathe of society feels the weight of ableism, racism, and capitalism. We can make different choices both structurally and interpersonally in terms of how we understand and make space for difference. The perils, yet also the beauty, of social construction is that where cultures become intentionally made by way of normalization; they can also be undone, unlearnt, and dismantled. We take the spirit of hope and change into this chapter to tap into a level of consciousness among our readers that we hope contains the will to change our society.

We frame this chapter through an eleven-point manifesto that provides an instructive and carefully considered round-up of the contentions and discussions presented throughout this book (a few new ones too!). Keeping the objective of exposing, deconstructing, and dismantling neurotypical hegemony at the forefront of this, we continue our structural and interpersonal analysis, which has been embedded in critical discussions centered on both love and hope. In this way, we recognize the need to take seriously how hegemony impacts our relationships and our daily lives, and this is, of course, also structurally informed. If we can take seriously how ableism can be reproduced even among the people who provide us with love and care, we can begin to see the issue as something that transcends individualism—something that is much more embedded in normative culture. This being said, we have also sought throughout the book to highlight the power of agency and collectives to disrupt these processes, as well as that the routes into addressing neurotypical hegemony are *multidirectional.*

In this multidirectional approach, first of all, we need to recognize that dismantling neurotypical hegemony requires the active participation of the neuromajority. This is foundational. Secondly, our multidirectional approach requires us to make clear that the instructive and personal slant of the book is also about contributing to discussions that encourage our neurodiverse siblings to continue to push for a place in society where they can "come as they are." The threads of hopefulness woven throughout signify that this book itself contributes to the growing volume of evidence that the deconstruction of neurotypical hegemony is becoming an active and necessary ingredient in the theory and praxis of all social justice movements.

Part of the reason why we feel it is important to summarize the arguments in this book in manifesto form is that to show how to intentionally dismantle neurotypical hegemony we need to be descriptive, illustrative, and concise. Consequently, we have presented our concluding remarks in the form of a list, to show exactly where and how we can make neurodivergence a normative aspect of contemporary society. As we have consistently argued throughout, neurotypical hegemony is harmful for everyone—even the neurotypical majority—and this instructive eleven-point manifesto is a demonstration of the critical but loving framework we envisage.[1]

1. Solidarity with Our Ageing Population

We have a global ageing population. According to the World Health Organization, the number of people aged sixty years and older in the population is increasing; by 2019 the number of people aged sixty and older was estimated to be one billion, a figure due to reach 1.4 billion by 2030 and 2.1 billion by 2050.[2] This growth in older populations is accelerating. We are not making this point to contribute in any way to racist and colonial discourses surrounding developing countries and childbirth, but more to make the point that this kind of demographic change requires social and structural changes which would also benefit the neurodiverse and disabled community.

Throughout the book, we have explored how disability rights, infused with an emphasis on racism, ableism, and capital provide routes to understanding how to create a solidarity-infused politics for everyone. In doing so, we have sought to demonstrate how the politics of neurodiversity can operate as a lens which takes seriously all social justice issues. While we have not spoken directly about this matter, we recognize in this concluding chapter that the multiple human emergencies currently felt on a global scale could rapidly be accounted for and responded to in loving ways if the elderly were understood as a group of people who require care.

If we create cultures that are actively loving of our ageing population, then we are already half way to recognizing and including neuro-minorities in a meaningful way. Both elderly and neurodivergent people often struggle to feel at peace in their bodies and brains, and the spaces in which they find themselves. The issues are sensory, physical, and practical; they are related to housing, access, and care. There are similarities between the politics of representation we have critiqued throughout the book and the way that people say they 'care' about old people. The reality is that it is not enough to simply make this statement—a discourse of care requires a more thoroughgoing and practical engagement with the sentiment.

As with many of our contentions, the primary issue here concerns the distribution of resources. There is enough global capital to allow elderly people to live well as they age, and to die in a dignified way. Similarly, there is enough global capital to allow all neurodivergent and neurotypical people to live a life that allows them to be safe, comfortable, and fulfilled. We draw a direct link between neurodivergence and age, not because we see either as hopeless, but rather because we see many correlations between ageism and ableism. Both groups experience the sharper end of neurotypical hegemony and must find similar ways to survive. What is clear, as with many of the discussions about resources and capital throughout the book is that elderly and neurodivergent people with greater access to resources have a much more straightforwardly linear relationship with neurotypical hegemony. We say this to illustrate—again—the realities of managing neurotypical hegemony in an intersectional way; put simply, some of the struggles we have explored in this book are neither evenly felt nor equitably distributed. A purely generational analysis is flawed, especially as we sit here thinking and writing in Britain, where we know that there are some very wealthy elderly people as well as many who live in poverty. According to the State of Ageing Report among UK adults,[3] people aged sixty to sixty-four now have the highest rate of relative poverty at twenty-five percent. More than one in three people from Bangladeshi and Pakistani backgrounds aged fifty and over are living in relative poverty.[4] As we write, the country is entering its fourteenth year under a system of austerity politics, which we know has disproportionately affected families with disabilities and the elderly. It is also pertinent to mention here the global COVID-19 pandemic that began in 2019, which also disproportionately impacted the disabled and elderly. To repeat—the issue here is one of social care. We emphasize this in the hope that of equipping readers with a point of reference to help explain the multifaceted and deeply political nature of neurodiversity. Solidarity between old people and the neurodiverse community is key.

2. Abolish Exams

In chapter 5, we outlined how the institution of education needs a complete rethink. We spoke critically about our own relationships with education and made clear that our position is that we should remove and abolish all exams. This is not only a disability issue, but also a matter of race and class. Many will see this stance, made from our position as educators, as somewhat hypocritical, which is a view we understand. But we feel that many of the issues in contemporary society can be located in this unquestioning emphasis on measurements that simply do not reflect an individual's capabilities. If someone performs well in exams, it is only a demonstration that they are well suited to a very particular form of thinking and learning.

As we explored in the chapter on schools and education, as a society we have lost any sense of what it means to engage in education and knowledge production in a meaningful and emancipatory way. Education should be about equipping members of civil society with the tools to understand themselves and others and helping them find out where they would like to contribute to society. Further, education is about learning how to interact in a multicultural society. When we lay out this system at its most basic, it becomes glaringly obvious that the way we measure and examine young people in schools has been inextricably tied to an ableist culture. Exams disproportionately produce disposable knowledge and cultures that dispose of people.

The global COVID-19 pandemic, when children did not attend school for long periods during lockdown, was one of the first moments at which the reductive nature of the metrics of education were widely exposed across the whole of neurotypical society. For the first time, young people of all classes and ethnicity were told that predictive grades would be used as reliable performance indicators. The winners and losers in this approach can be understood through the lenses of disability, race, gender, and class, but the point we wish to make here is that this set an important precedent that showed just how subjective the system of measurement of neurotypical education has been to date. However, society remains wedded to common sense ideas about education and value as natural, despite the fact that they are constructed. But while we know that recognizing a politics of neurodiversity in education makes us susceptible to a neo-liberal culture that commodifies disability, we see proposals for the reform of exams as a red herring. Exams need to be abolished.

3. End Speed Over Process

We must slow down communications and revise our expectations of engagement for all people. Whether we are speaking in person, in groups, online, at work or in the home, we need to review the way we communicate. This is not as simple as "slowing down" but more about checking in with people on whether they are comfortable with the way information is being presented. Are everyone's needs being met? Is there space for people to express miscommunication? In many ways this point could be positioned as one of our more interpersonally infused interventions. It's a personal one for us! We recognize that conditions might not always allow for this instruction to take place. But in general, we do stress the need for us to *slow down*. By slowing down our communication we will find opportunities to learn. Crucially, this is all centered around the notion of speed over process, which is one of the main issues we observe in neurotypical society.

This can be best expressed by pointing to the fact that in all aspects of our personal and professional lives, pace and our ability to endure multiple intensities has become the norm. Our lives have become bound, both by productivity and by our capacity to be as efficient as a possible. Crucially, this emphasis on speed transcends our working lives and has found its way into our personal and intimate social relations. Never has it been more apparent that capitalism has infected our relationships and our communities. And when we consider what speed has done to our personal and professional lives, we are mainly concerned with the space—or rather the lack of it—allocated to understanding and communicating with each other. Put simply, neurodivergent people need space to register what is happening and how to respond in everyday life. This is not because we are in any way lacking, many of us simply have different ways of communicating how we feel. But the parameters of communication and understanding have been set by the neurotypical hegemony we have outlined throughout this book. Dismantling neurotypical hegemony means abolishing the value we assign to speed over process, and as with all the arguments we have made concerning neurodivergent inclusivity, we see a critical evaluation of all social processes as emancipatory for everyone in society. A rejection of the current emphasis on speed could be beneficial for everyone. Speed is the orthodoxy to which we are all subjected. The neurodivergent community is often at the more difficult end of this experience, continually oscillating between two worlds, of which one is a world shaped by adaptability, where the other is shaped by an imposed assimilation into neurotypical society, often as a state of survival. It is particularly challenging to try to understand this, given the absence of tolerance in our society (sponsored by speed!). Neurotypical people sometimes struggle to understand neurodiverse behaviors and consequently our neurodivergent reality. A lifetime of containment (and not being ourselves) can consume our lived experience.

Even if we are unable to convince the neurotypical majority of the perils of speed, we know that for the vast majority of people their personal relationships are fundamental to their lives. What if we told you that speed could be a primary reason why relationships breakdown? We see speed as synonymous with miscommunication, misunderstanding, and conflict. Although we understand conflict as an essential part of social life, and an aspect of how we come to understand each other, we see that the value attributed to speed is something that thwarts our capacity to reconcile.

4. Neurodivergent People Are Part of Society

Though we have filled much of this book with discussions of the impact of neurotypical hegemony on the whole of society, it is still important to reflect on how we socially construct neurodiversity. We must continue to work towards recognizing neurodivergent people as part of society. Neurodivergent people and the cultures they produces *are* society. Neurotypical hegemony has a negative impact on everyone—not just those who are neurodiverse—but we still need to recognize that it overwhelmingly marginalizes the lives of those who are neurodivergent and disabled. We must continue to prompt ourselves and our readers to keep thinking critically about how to create spaces where difference is accepted and not just tolerated.

5. Ending Speed Over Process (continued): The Workplace

During the global COVID-19 pandemic, our good friend and sister Paulette Williams spoke very powerfully about what the lockdowns meant for the workplace and for the education system specifically. In Paulette's words, the global response to this emergency showed us very simply that nothing is set, everything can be changed and our processes are not fixed. And with this we return to another crucial conduit for ending speed over process—the workplace. The custom of speed over process has been so deeply embedded in so much of our lives that speed has become a marker of competence. Crucially, this shapes many of our daily experiences in the workplace. Speaking here as neurodivergent people who have strived to assimilate, the workplace has always been a conundrum for us. As work remains central to how we come to live and relate to each other, the workplace is an essential element in our manifesto for change. Despite spending much of our working lives frustrated by the cultures it promotes and accepts, it has always been an intriguing phenomenon that simultaneously provides fulfilment and frustration. These are clearly feelings and emotions that transcend the neurodivergent experience. Modes of interaction, and how they may unconsciously or consciously exclude particular people, remain a seminal part of the difficulty of establishing a sense of belonging at work. The workplace operates on a membership system, part of which involves the recognition of particular types of capital as currency. Overwhelmingly, the gold standard of capital in the workplace is an individual's ability to assimilate into neurotypical culture. Speed is a secondary, but also deeply embedded, element of neurotypical culture. It is a form of currency that is—possibly—seen as of the highest value. Of course, speed is not a determinant of competence but it is regarded as an important facet in the capitalistic, neo-liberal ecosystem. It can be the difference between making or not making friends, and even in whether you are valued by your employer. Speed appears to trump cohesive relationships and is constantly valued above employee relatability. If you can understand things fast enough, you are almost guaranteed to be a valued member of staff. Our primary point here is that speed needs to be removed from our understanding of both work and value. Of course it marginalizes neurodivergent people, but it sets parameters that create stressful and challenging cultures for neurotypical people too.

This emphasis on speed disregards other ways of being and knowing and situates neurotypical hegemony as *efficiency*. Accommodating other forms of knowledge production, or neurodiversity, has been a marginal consideration for workplace culture. Consequently, reasonable adjustments are often an afterthought, meaning that neurodivergent people are judged against an orthodoxy that is discriminatory, exclusionary, and generally problematic in terms of maximizing the productivity of individuals in the labor market. Crucially, these are cultures that make life difficult for everyone.

For both of us the workplace has proven to be a challenging place. The way that competence and intellect are framed have not been particularly affirming or positive reference points. Such experiences leave residual feelings of inadequacy that reaffirm dominant myths regarding the capabilities of neurodivergent and disabled people in the workplace. This sense of permanently residing on the margins becomes further exacerbated the longer it goes on, contributing to a state of *assimilation fatigue.* The codeswitching required becomes exhausting and inevitably compromises psychological wellbeing, given the expectation for neurodivergent people to comply, conceal, suppress, or adjust behavioral traits that may not be deemed socially acceptable. Belonging in the workplace therefore becomes the province of the able-bodied and the neurotypical, resembling an entitlement and an embodied privilege that operates through mechanisms of exclusion.

Our manifesto posits a workplace dialogue situated in equity, empathy, and understanding. This is what neurodivergent individuals need to establish a sense of belonging and stability in what has otherwise been—historically—a hostile and exclusionary space. Understanding the evolving nature of disability discrimination in the workplace—and how it subtly pervades everything—is of interest to everyone, given the collective benefits of developing more accommodating workspaces for everyone.

We now want to suggest that we invest (as a society) in producing work cultures that prioritize process, patterns, and repetition. Neurodivergent people often rely on patterns and repetition; they are very methodical. Part of that attention to detail and process is how we keep ourselves safe, and one of the aspects of neurodiversity we have addressed as both liberatory and hopeful comes from some of the strategies we use to manage our everyday lives in neurotypical society.

Patience—emails and deadlines.
Tolerance - the way we engage in instruction.
People get impatient with how methodical I am.

Processes are so important.
Because I don't want to make a mistake.
We need to deconstruct time—Lewis and Arday (2023)

6. Make Transport Safer

Chantelle: On a summer's day in Oxford in August 2023, I was waiting for Jason to arrive for a writing session. For me, train stations have often been sites of frustration. Many service workers at stations are underpaid, which can breed sentiments of distrust and impatience with the general public (see chapter 5). This is a culture that can be seen in a lot of staffed public places. Our recognition, at this point, that service workers are underpaid—is an attempt to acknowledge, understand and empathize. As neurodivergent people, these environments are some of the most disorientating we encounter. As I stood on the platform, I looked to my left and saw a woman in distress being searched by the British Transport Police. The woman was short and wore glasses. Within ten seconds it was clear to me that she was disabled. I stood next to the scene, approximately fifteen feet from the police and the woman. When I see multiple police officers inside the physical and personal space of a citizen, I always do my best to stand nearby in support of the citizen in question. On this occasion, as on others, one of the officers approached me and asked me not to stand and stare at them. I said, truthfully, that I was waiting for a friend, at which they asked me not to be hostile. As Black and neurodivergent people, when we see someone like ourselves in a situation that has the possibility to become criminalizing, our hearts so often drop. We understand what is happening and know that it is incredibly challenging for someone to communicate what they need when they are at their most distressed. Public spaces can be massively disorientating, and the trend towards the presence of staff whose purpose is simply to monitor and criminalize makes them even more challenging. With a combination of greater use of artificial intelligence, alongside staff whose role is to ensure that rules are followed, train stations have become a particularly tense experience. As I watched the police search and question the woman, I could not help but think how a lack of sustainable advocacy and support for neurodivergent and disabled people in public spaces can make the difference between successfully boarding a train and being arrested. In that situation, I could not even guarantee that a neurodivergent person would understand that I wanted to help them or be certain that she would understand that the police were being heavy-handed with her simply because she is disabled and does not have a clear community of support around her. As I fixated on the injustice transpiring, I thought about the context of the train station, the process of buying a ticket, looking at the time of your train and getting on your train. There are so many variables to consider. On a bad day, the overstimulation caused by the environment of the station, followed by a wrong turn or a sudden and disorientating movement make us more likely to be in this woman's situation. As we explored earlier, speed over process can be deadly for neurodivergent people using public services in a society that does not value its workers; disabled people are more likely to experience the impatience and lack of compassion bred by this. This is why freedom and care for all are at the heart of our manifesto and embedded in the cultures we would like to establish.

Many of the disability rights activists we cite throughout this book have been at the forefront of conversations and critical interventions on the rise of artificial intelligence and lack of human contact in public spaces. As public services have become privatized, so has the movement of people. Neurotypical society assumes that everyone understands what is going on everywhere, but collective movements of people in spaces like train stations exemplify precisely what we are trying to critique and dismantle. As public service funding continues to be discontinued, and public spaces are privatized, these are spaces that have become incredibly challenging and unsafe for neurodivergent people. An increase in staff presence across all public spaces would enable people both to understand and to find their bearings when experiencing overstimulation.

7. Emotion and Patience

We need to create more acceptance and understanding that people digest the rollercoaster that is everyday social life in different ways; many of the ordinary moments that we are referring to require an emphasis on emotional responses to confrontation, anger, disappointments, surprises, romantic love, and parenting. We use the word emotional here not to project any kind of negative label onto emotion per se, or the state of emotionality, or to promote what some might deem to be "emotionless" behavior, but more to mark its integral yet changeable use across society. People live inside their own subjectivity, and their emotions usually map on to a variety of existing life experiences, their families, the people they are in community with, and of course, their proximity to neurodivergence. The seventh point in our manifesto refers to the recognition that we need—intentionally—to make more space and have greater patience for understanding emotions across the whole of society.

There is a general assumption that the ways in which the structures of society affect our sense of self should have a universal set of responses. Here we are primarily referring to the fact that what is called emotional dysregulation is a central feature of living as a neurodivergent person, and this feature of our manifesto is about centering awareness that emotion, and how it is received (and hopefully accepted), needs to be approached with both compassion and understanding. In an ableist society we see the life courses of disabled and neurodivergent people as producing an ongoing battle with our emotions as we attempt to manage them when we are overstimulated. In the section on transport, above, we explored how a shortage of staff has become a permanent risk for neurodivergent people and others at risk of episodes of mental ill-health. How we construct the ideal emotional response across society is a constant concern for neurodivergent people. Recognizing the parameters of what is considered a reasonable emotional response can be extremely challenging for neurodivergent people in neurotypical society. We need to get better at recognizing the plurality of responses to contemporary social issues and environments.

8. Shifting Our Cultures through Civic Responsibility

As members of civil society, we have a civic responsibility to challenge the way our society treats disabled people. We see this as a process of collective reimagination which requires humility, honesty, and space for learning. As we look towards other social movements that have coalesced around issues related to the materiality of social life, race, and gender, we see that some of the biggest challenges within these groups have been the overemphasis on the question of doing the "right" thing. We are so often fixated on who has the most productive course of action in response to the question of how we get free. Some want us to engage with a politics that is resistant to understanding difference, whereas others tend to recommend fixed ideas about who should be central to the production of ideas and knowledge about the ways we get free. Our approach is multifaceted and embedded in the unknowing of social life and recognition of the role of both structure and agency. Simply put, we all need space to make mistakes and learn together. We also need to make space for ourselves in ways that acknowledge our own humanity, but not at the expense of others.

This point is about how we understand different people and experiences, and about how the lack of time dedicated to this facet of social life is essential to the social reproduction of neurotypical hegemony. The ways that people are stratified along the lines of disability, race, and class produce cultures resistant to love and care. By creating cultures that align value with productivity we are failing to appreciate people's needs, while centering the requirements of capitalist production. Consequently, we now stress that a plurality of care requires a more supple and agile way of understanding all people. Our culture and social values need to better reflect a civic duty to recognize disability, not as a marginal issue but as one that has its roots in equity for all. This change cannot be one that underestimates the impact of attitudes.

9. Democratizing Sustainable Access to Resources

Throughout the arguments in this book, we have continued to turn back to the idea that neurotypical hegemony functions to preserve capitalism and the consequences of this are primarily found in the materiality of everyday life. Effectively, the materiality of everyday life is determined by how much money we can access to pay for shelter, food, and care at all stages of life. The materiality of everyday life is the connection between social and economic safety and security (or lack of). In this way, sustained access to resources and support can bridge the difference between the unliveable and liveability across all societies. In 2024, as we write this, we continue to live in a society which is experiencing a global emergency involving access to resources across all intersections. Here in Britain, when it comes to disability, geographies of inequality largely dictate who is able to access a more ordinary and dignified existence. Justine Karpusheff of the Health Foundation, notes that these geographies of inequality are best captured by what has become known as a "postcode lottery." She uses this notion to demonstrate the wide disparities in health and social care services in different parts of the country, and how the area in which you are born, raised, or live can affect your well-being.[5] Here, disability justice remains an urgent issue for policy makers at both geographic and demographic levels.[6] While the north-south divide remains relevant at local (i.e., national) level, here in Britain as well as globally, the urgent call for place-based responses to inequity remains a vital aspect of all our social justice movements.[7] Our leaders need to work more closely with local communities to understand people's social and material needs in a more holistic and intentional way. At their core, place-based responses to access and resources are centered around ways to create more democratic advice and interventions on all matters related to social care.

10. Race and Class Together as Central to the Neurodiversity Movement

Understanding race and class in tandem and together must be an essential part of the neurodiversity movement. We have to play close attention to the intersectional nature of neurodiversity and be intentional about recognizing that ableism is not evenly felt or experienced among the disability community. We reject the idea of a "race to the bottom" when it comes to how we understand the prevalence of inequality in society, yet we must continue to do the messy work of outlining the ways that race and class have a demonstrable impact on the treatment of all people.

We cannot truly understand how race is socially produced without looking at class and we cannot adequately represent class politics without an understanding of race. It is no longer reasonable for the disability and neurodiversity movement to treat race and class as an add-on to our calls for action and advocacy. Throughout the book, we have stressed that the connections between racism, ableism, and capitalism are crucial to the way neurotypical hegemony is upheld. We have stressed that the structural formations of society, which cut across multiple intersecting lines, urgently need to be addressed if we are to truly achieve inclusive cultures of difference. If we do not make clear the importance of race and class in how we imagine and create more equitable societies then we have simply agreed to the politics of representation being enough for our movement.

In 2023, after the publication of our *Sociological Review* paper on Blackness, neurodiversity, and higher education, we received many emails and messages from fellow neurodivergent people who were moved by the following words, which were spoken by Jason, and which we quoted in our paper:

As we see more representation of neurodiversity entering the public domain it all feels very celebratory which is great, but we never actually spoke about what it means? We are celebrating it before we have actually spoken about it. So we are saying we are celebrating something that you don't understand. You don't understand how people navigate neurodiversity and you haven't actually changed any of your processes and we still use the same idea of the same glove fits everyone. (Jason Arday, 2022)

Here, Jason was drawing on the importance of understanding the actual lived experience of neurodivergent individuals as they navigate social life. We highlighted the importance of this in chapter 1, where we provided our more nuanced perspective on the politics of representation as in some cases delaying the structural work required to redress ableism. We recognize that a way to move beyond this omission (the absence of discussion about what navigating neurodivergence is actually like), could be more easily achieved if we joined causes with those seeking to address the perils of racism and capitalism. So many of our needs and desires as people and as a society can be traced to the way the slippery and temporal evolution of race has been and continues to be used to justify class inequity. By continuing to uphold the idea that racial difference creates a "natural" order in society, we are allowing the divisions between different groups of people—all of whom may be looking for very similar access to resources—to remain intact. Combining our movement with movements for social justice for race, class, and disability is the only way we will truly get to grips with the varying but overlapping needs of the most marginalized in society. By attending to the needs of the most marginalized and vulnerable, we will automatically create cultures and a politics that will benefit everyone, regardless of their position in society. Looking after and supporting the most vulnerable, and freedom for us all, is within touching distance.

11. Valuing Time

"CJ, the most valuable gift in this life is time."

—JASON

One of life's biggest gifts is time, and one of its biggest challenges is also time. Time is something that can be given and taken. As neurodivergent scholars who belong to the global Black diaspora the concept of time is deeply embedded in how we come to understand ourselves and everyday life. Many of our ancestors had time stripped away from them via the violent extractions of slavery, colonial expansion, and empire. But many of them also resisted by reclaiming time through our long histories of community organizing against state-led marginalization. From radical political education to government lobbying, striking, and the Black Parents movement,[8] so much of our history of resistance has required us to reclaim time taken from us. Marginalizing people on the basis of their race and class position is rooted in the extraction of their time; time to be free, ordinary and live a dignified life.

The abstraction of time from so many groups whose struggle is embedded in movements for social justice is central to the dominating features of neurotypical hegemony. We are living and working in a system where time is often one of the first components of liveability taken away from people. Here we pay close attention to how, historically speaking, time has been used as a way to remove ordinariness and dignity from people's lives. The removal of time, in particular, has been used to uphold the structures of ableism, racism, and capitalism. We now want to make clear that providing, giving, and making space for people to more freely access time is what will help us to redress structural inequity. Our positioning of time here should not be confused with the delay, the waiting for, or even the pausing of interventions to redress inequity. Time is what is needed for the framework of love and hope to uphold. We urgently need the time and space to individually and collectively heal from what we have described throughout this book, and the ways for us to do this require us to learn more about the practical, intellectual, and spiritual tools needed to love ourselves and each other. We need more demonstrations of love and care from those who hold the keys to access resources. They—just as much as we—need to work on valuing time in a way that becomes synonymous with our own well-being. From meditation to exercise; from documenting our thoughts to talking therapies, to being outside with nature—all these require us to value time in a way that prioritizes inner work as an essential component of creating our own versions of ordinariness and dignity.

Time to heal, time to understand and time to imagine more equitable futures for us all. Intentionally valuing time creates courage, compassion and connection.

Talking about a Revolution or Behind the Wall? Educationally Subnormal Schools in Britain

They're talking about a revolution?
It sounds like a whisper
Don't you know
Talking about a revolution?
It sounds like a whisper

(TRACY CHAPMAN, 1989)

Last night I heard the screaming
Loud voices behind the wall
Another sleepless night for me

(TRACY CHAPMAN, 1988)

For any music fan who draws inspiration from consciousness-raising lyrics, it will be no surprise that we have decided to end our book with Tracy Chapman. Known for her social activism and her feminist endeavors, Chapman has spent much of her career advocating for human rights and notes that her role has primarily been focused on fundraising and raising awareness of global inequalities. This final, short chapter takes inspiration from two song titles from the self-titled album *Tracy Chapman*. One of these songs is dedicated to the possibilities of making change, and the other explores the painful realities of domestic violence and abuse.

In early 2024, the writer, audio producer, and arts programmer Tej Adeleye contacted us about a project she was leading, based on platforming the lives and experiences of Black adults in Britain who were sent as children to Educationally Subnormal schools (ESN schools) in the 1970s. Tej's work and activism has been an inspiring conduit for the arguments in this book. We are particularly grateful for her creative and authoritative work in and with the community, in which she has sought to democratize the archives and oral histories of the social justice movements of the past to inform the present. Tej's work is an example of the fusion and possibilities of music, history, and society in creating the neurodivergent modes of communicating we discussed in chapter 2. As a Black woman who received her neurodivergence diagnosis as an adult, Tej has been on a mission to look at the histories of racism and ableism and how her own experiences map onto the ongoing perils of neurotypical hegemony. We incorporate her wisdoms at the end of this book, as her work is a prime example of the application of the Afrocentric feminist epistemologies of Patricia Hill Collins. She has used her lived experience of racism and ableism to contribute to retelling the histories of the neurodiversity movement. We are grateful to Tej for prompting us to recognize that incidents of racism and ableism in tandem need greater representation and understanding in the disability and neurodiversity movement if we are to be truly inclusive. At this point, we need to offer a short introduction to the cultural, social, and historical backdrop that informs this concluding point on the importance of the ESN schools.

The term "educationally subnormal" was originally used in the 1944 Education Act in England and Wales. At that time, it was the responsibility of teachers to recommend whether children should be sent to ESN schools. The introduction of this legislation can be understood as an intervention made by the government, who after World War Two, who were looking more closely at the trends reported amongst child development and child psychiatry research. Of course, we are grateful for the scholars mentioned throughout this book, like Robert Chapman, who reminds us of the harms caused historically by the discipline and institutional formations of psychiatry, and the psych disciplines more broadly.[1] But playing close attention here to the treatment of Black children specifically, we can begin to see how concern with the lives of children deemed "intellectually deficient" became a moral panic, and created a culture of institutional harm and neglect. Crucially, this was a racist culture justified through the enactment of state ableism.

In 1960s and 1970s Britain, Black children were disproportionately sent to schools designated for children labelled "educationally subnormal."[2] A 1967 report by the Inner London Education Authority found that twenty-eight percent of children in ESN schools in London were black immigrant children, in comparison with fifteen percent of the mainstream school population.[3] In the late 1960s, Bernard Coard, a PhD student working in ESN schools, was outraged by the disproportionate number of Black immigrant and Caribbean children being sent to the ESN schools. With the publication of his ground-breaking book *How the West Indian Child Is Made Educationally Sub-Normal in the British School System*, Coard was able to publicize the concerns of the Black Parents movement and give voice to the racism and ableism embodied in the ESN schools (see also chapter 4). Just ten years later, the sociologist of education and inequality, Sally Tomlinson, published *Educational Subnormality: A study in decision-making*, in which she reported that Black children were being referred and moved to ESN schools more speedily than white or South Asian children.[4] She interviewed headteachers, who seldom hid their racist and ableist beliefs, and told her that West Indian children were likely to be slow at learning, have poor concentration, speak Creole dialect, be volatile, boisterous, extrovert and troublesome, and have family problems and working mothers. It would be fifty years before the experiences of Black and immigrant children would be portrayed in a less pejorative and more mainstream way—in an episode of Steve McQueen's *Small Axe* TV drama anthology series, *Education*.

More research remains to be done on the harms caused by the institutionalization of Black and indigenous people of color and disabled people on a global scale, if we are to truly understand our shared histories of struggle, learn from the past, and make space to be accountable to lost generations of people. Tej has managed to interview several of the Black adults who were sent to ESN schools and has documented the work one of the producers of BBC Radio 4's Sideways podcast, Divergent Histories.[5] As we talked together about what she has uncovered, she spoke of the lives ruined by these schools. Much of the testimony consists of accounts of lifetimes of mental distress and feelings of unworthiness. After the TV drama, *Education*, filmmaker Lyttana Shannon and Steve McQueen followed up with a documentary entitled *Subnormal: A British Scandal* (May 2021), which focused on first person accounts and stories of the lives of those who experienced this atrocity.[6]

Returning to the present day, as we conclude this book we remain grateful to the work of parents, activists and academics who have dedicated time to bringing miscarriages of educational justice to public attention. But in our own very small contributions to democratizing these histories, we can see just how much work still needs to be done to highlight the importance of embedding—in both historical and present-day examples of racism and the harms of capitalism—our struggle for disability justice. We have been invited to speak at a variety of public and academic discussions about neurodiversity and we now try to make a point of addressing the existence of ESN schools as crucial for our understanding of the development of the neurodiversity and disability movement. When we have delivered talks to institutions and organizations primarily founded on the premise of neurodiversity, we have been surprised to learn how little is known about the ESN schools and the disproportionately racialized exclusion and treatment of Black children. Similarly, when we have spoken about the histories of the psych disciplines with psych communities, we have learnt how little is known or understood about this history.

In 2023, a group of Black Britons hired a solicitor and began legal action against the British government over the label "educationally subnormal." They are demanding a formal apology and compensation from the government.[7] Speaking to *The Voice*, their solicitor, Frances Swaine, who is leading the campaign on behalf of those affected, said

> I represent people whose entire lives have been shaped by the fact that as children they were wrongly labeled as educationally subnormal, a label that was disproportionately applied to African and Caribbean children in the 1960s and 70s. These people have suffered the terrible consequences of

this labeling for their whole lives. The classification was a result of racism in education that still continues today.[8]

We see this quote and the move towards legal action as a practical example of the love, hope, and solidarity we advocate. *Love* as a way of seeking redress for historical harms, *hope* that practical steps are being taken to give voice to these injustices, and *solidarity* as something that can be seen in this process, in which multiple parties and institutions are making these cases public. We also see how activism requires the participation of people from a range of different walks of life and professions to increase the potential for restorative justice. This overlap between the Black Parents movement of previous decades, the careful and diligent democratizing work of Tej Adeleye, and the legal action of people labelled ESN as children, demonstrates the size of the challenge and the length of time it may take.

In these final pages of our rallying call to dismantle neurotypical hegemony, the reverberation of Tracy Chapman's "Talking About a Revolution" and "Behind the Wall" resonate with many of our contentions throughout this book. Through the lens of neurodiversity, we have embarked on a journey of understanding, empathy, and empowerment. With the examples of the ESN schools in this Afterword, and much like Tracy Chapman's "Talking About a Revolution," the book underscores the importance of dialogue and activism in challenging stigma and fostering inclusion. Crucially, there is a need for us all to understand our complex social histories. Moreover, the poignant strains of Chapman's "Behind the Wall" serve as a backdrop to the personal stories shared, which formed the basis of our inspiration for this book and shed light on the barriers and isolation experienced by neurodivergent and disabled individuals.

What we hope can be taken from this book is that amongst the challenges of a society culturally and socially entrenched in ableism, racism, and capitalism there emerge spirits of resilience and hope. Much like the spirited call for change in "Talking About a Revolution," our book champions the voices of neurodiverse individuals and their allies who dare to challenge the status quo. It celebrates the courage to speak out, to demand recognition, and to forge pathways toward inclusivity and justice. Yet, intertwined with this anthem of resilience is the haunting melody of "Behind the Wall," a reminder of the barriers and isolation that still pervade our society. The struggles depicted in that song mirror the experiences of many individuals, confronting invisible walls erected by ignorance and prejudice.

But we still lean on the possibilities of love and hope and take solace in the stories we constantly hear of resistance to inequity, which demonstrate that these chapters are not just narratives of struggle but also narratives of triumph—testaments to the resilience and beauty of neurodiversity.

In closing, let us carry forward the spirit of Tracy Chapman's songs—a commitment to continue "Talking about a Revolution" and breaking down the walls that divide us. May our journey through these pages serve as a catalyst for greater understanding, compassion, and genuine inclusion in our communities and beyond.

NOTES

Preface: Come as You Are

1. Chopra, Deepak. "The Soul of Healing Affirmations."
2. Schwartz-Johnston, "Ableism, Personhood, and Communication for People Who Don't Speak."
3. Loja et al., "Disability, Embodiment and Ableism: Stories of Resistance."
4. The title of the book is a lyric from the 1994 Oasis song, "Live Forever." The song lyrics are used to pay homage to Jason's mother (Gifty Arday) who used music to help him to understand social interactions. We intended this lyric—with the word "never"—to be read as symbolic rather than literal. We do not intend to describe these discussions as determined, but rather to stress how our neurodivergent ways of being, living, and thinking transcend neurotypicality.
5. Oasis was an English rock band formed in Manchester, England in 1991. Originally known as the Rain, the group initially consisted of Liam Gallagher (lead vocals, tambourine), Paul Arthurs (guitar), Paul McGuigan (bass guitar) and Tony McCarroll (drums), with Liam's older brother Noel (lead guitar, vocals) joining as a fifth member a few months after their formation. They went through various changes in membership, with the Gallagher brothers the only consistently present members.

Chapter 1: Sowing the Seeds of Love

1. Radulski, "Conceptualising Autistic Masking," 120.
2. hooks, *Outlaw Culture*, 293.
3. Maté, *Scattered Minds*.
4. Kumari Campbell, "Exploring Internalized Ableism," 151.
5. Kumari Campbell, "Exploring Internalized Ableism," 155.
6. Brissett-Bailey, *Black, Brilliant and Dyslexic*.
7. Chapman, "Neurodiversity Theory and Its Discontents."
8. Chapman, "Neurodiversity Theory and Its Discontents," 371.

9. The medical model sees a person's impairment as the cause of their disability, tending to view it as resulting from their physical or mental limitations and not as connected to their social or geographical environments.

10. Burawoy, "For Public Sociology."

11. hooks, *All about Love*, 53.

12. Chapman, *Empire of Normality*, 15.

13. See https://leadingroutes.org/

14. hooks, *All about Love*, 220.

15. Noor and Shafee, "The role of critical friends in action research," 1.

16. hooks, *Feminism Is for Everybody*.

17. The Equality Trust.

18. Alston, "Statement on Visit to the United Kingdom."

19. Booth, "UK 'in Violation of International Law.'"

20. Statista.com. "Wealth Distribution in the United States in the Third Quarter of 2023," Accessed December 20, 2023.

21. Dorling, *Do We Need Economic Inequality?*

22. Diemer et al., "Autism Presentation in Female and Black Populations."

23. Cooper, *Eloquent Rage*.

24. For example, Genius Within is a UK based organization dedicated to celebrating and championing neurodiversity, "Working towards a future where all neurominorities will be able to maximize their potential and work to their strengths." https://geniuswithin.org/our-team/.

25. Goodley et al., "Feeling Disability"; see also Thomas, *Female Forms*.

26. Dyi Huijg, "Neuronormativity in Theorising Agency," 215.

27. Gramsci, *Selections from the Prison Notebooks*.

28. Channel Four describes *The Undatables* as follows: "People living with challenging conditions are often considered 'undateable'—this series meets a few and follows their attempts to find love."

29. *Love on the Spectrum* is a documentary following the lives of young adults on the autism spectrum as they explore the unpredictable world of love, dating, and relationships. https://www.imdb.com/title/tt11904786/.

30. Hill Collins, *Black Feminist Thought, 30th Anniversary Edition*.

31. Young, "What Is Black British Feminism?"; Beverley et al., *The Heart of the Race*; Ngcobo, ed., *Let It Be Told*.

32. Sobande, *The Digital Lives of Black Women in Britain*.

33. Reynolds, "Re-thinking a Black Feminist Standpoint."

34. hooks, *Outlaw Culture*, 290.

35. See also Brown, Ashkenazy, and Morenike, eds. *All the Weight of Our Dreams: on Living Racialized Autism*.

36. Bailkin, *The Afterlife of Empire*.

37. Lange, *Lineages of Despotism and Development*, 123.

38. Fanon, *The Wretched of the Earth*.

39. Fanon, *The Wretched of the Earth*, 42.

40. Hall, "Whites of Their Eyes."

41. Dodd, "Black People Nine Times More Likely to Face Stop and Search than White People."

42. Mundasad, "Black Women Four Times More Likely to Die in Childbirth."

43. Institute of Race Relations.

44. Mohdin and Gentleman, "UK Failing to Address Systemic Racism against Black People."

45. Lewis and Arday, "We'll See Things They'll Never See."

46. Robinson, *Black Marxism*.

47. Kumari Campbell, "Inciting Legal Fictions."

48. Lentin, *Why Race Still Matters*, 5.

49. Wilson, *Golden Gulag*, 28.

Chapter 2: What's Love Got to Do with It?

1. Morrison, *The Bluest Eye*, 110–130.

2. For an analysis of Hill Collins' four dimensions, see Kristal Moore Clemons, "Black Feminist Thought and Qualitative Research in Education."

3. Alexander, *Action and Its Environments*; Durkheim, *The Division of Labor*; Giddens, *Central Problems in Social Theory*.

4. Archer, *Structure, Agency and the Internal Conversation*. See especially the introduction.

5. Stenning and Bertilsdotter Rosqvist, "Neurodiversity Studies."

6. Brown, "Brené with Lisa Lahey on Immunity to Change."

7. Butler, *Frames of War*.

8. Meer and Holmwood, "John Holmwood: Sociology of Structure, Sociology as Structure."

9. See in particular, Maté, *Scattered Minds*.

10. Marx, *The Eighteenth Brumaire of Louis Bonaparte*.

11. Elder-Vass, *The Causal Power of Social Structures*, 3.

12. Bertilsdotter Rosqvist et al., "Naming Ourselves, Becoming Neurodivergent Scholars."

13. hooks, *All about Love*, 114.

14. Hill Collins, "Black Feminist Thought in the Matrix of Domination," 5–1.

15. hooks, *Teaching to Transgress*.

16. Back, "Why Everyday Life Matters."

17. Goodley et al., "Feeling Disability."

18. Goodley, "Dis/entangling Critical Disability Studies," 640.

19. Gorton, "Theorizing Emotion and Affect."

20. Wong, *Disability Visibility*.

21. Fanon, *The Wretched of the Earth*.

22. This term was coined by American sociologist C. Wright Mills in his 1959 book *The Sociological Imagination*. Mills was seeking to show how the discipline of sociology could offer wider insights into the connection between private and public life. He wrote that the sociological imagination allows the thinker to understand the wider historical context and understand its importance for the "inner" personal lives of those within that context. The sociological imagination is a way of thinking and analysis that asks us to step outside the limitations of our individual experiences and consider how our individual lives are connected to historical formations of society.

23. Hill Collins, *Black Feminist Thought: Knowledge, Consciousness, and the Politics of Empowerment*.

Chapter 3: I'll See You on the Dark Side of the Moon

1. Langenhoven et al., "The Psychosocial Personality Development of Syd Barrett."

2. Campanella, "Syd Barrett: Was He Suffering from Schizophrenia or Asperger's Syndrome?"

3. Lundberg and Chen, "Structural Ableism in Public Health and Healthcare."

4. Runswick-Cole, "'Us' and 'Them.'"

5. Sobande, *Consuming Crisis: Commodifying Care and COVID-19*.

6. Pickens, *Black Madness:: Mad Blackness*.

7. Goodley, "Towards Socially Just Pedagogies."

8. Aubrecht, "Disability Studies and the Language of Mental Illness."

9. Tyler, *Stigma: The Machinery of Inequality*.

10. Titchkosky, "Disability: A Rose by any Other Name?"

11. Aubrecht, "Disability Studies and the Language of Mental Illness," 4.

12. Radulski, "Conceptualising Autistic Masking."

13. Cage and Troxell-Whitman, "Understanding the Reasons, Contexts and Costs of Camouflaging."

14. Shaw et al., "Emotion Dysregulation in Attention Deficit Hyperactivity Disorder," 276.

15. Shaw et al., "Emotion Dysregulation in Attention Deficit Hyperactivity Disorder."

16. Pollak et al., "Symptoms of ADHD Predict Lower Adaptation to the COVID-19 Outbreak," 735.

17. Stewart et al., "Presentation of Depression in Autism and Asperger Syndrome."

18. Kõlves et al., "Assessment of Suicidal Behaviors Among Individuals with Autism Spectrum Disorder in Denmark."

19. Hedley et al., "Recommendations from the 2021 Australasian Society for Autism Research."

20. Lam, "Attention Deficit Disorder and Hospitalization." See also Rohn et al., "Adolescents Who Attempt Suicide."

21. Hinshaw, "Prospective Follow-Up of Girls with Attention-Deficit/Hyperactivity Disorder."

22. https://www.gla.ac.uk/news/archiveofnews/2022/september/headline _881944_en.html.

23. Durkheim, *Suicide*.

24. Selvin, "Durkheim's Suicide: Further Thoughts on a Methodological Classic"; Poppel and Day, "A Test of Durkheim's Theory of Suicide."

25. Bailey et al., "Self-harm in Young People."

26. Berger and Luckmann, *The Social Construction of Reality*.

27. World Health Organization, "Mental Health and Substance Use."

28. Naghavi et al., "Global, Regional, and National Burden of Suicide Mortality, 1990 to 2016."

29. On diagnoses of neurodiversity, we recommend the following: Johnson, "Neuroqueer Feminism"; Swartz, "Feminism and Psychiatric Diagnosis"; Metzl, *The Protest Psychosis*; Mollow, "'when Black women start going on Prozac.'"

30. Coker et al., "Racial and Ethnic Disparities in ADHD Diagnosis and Treatment."

31. Grant, "Neurodivergent Black Girls Don't Get the Same Help."

32. Patterson, "Nia's Autism Story."

33. Dunkley et al. "Overcrowded Specialist Schools." See also Eley and Holt. "Families of Disabled People tell BBC of Battle for NHS Care support."

34. https://www.perfectpop.org/.

35. Sinclair, "Don't Mourn for Us."

Chapter 4: The Great Beyond

1. Freire, *Pedagogy of the Oppressed*.

2. Chapman, *Empire of Normality*, 17.

3. Lewis and Kerkhoff-Parnell "Conceptualising Black (Co-)Reflexive Feminist Methodologies."

4. hooks, *Teaching to Transgress*, 19.

5. Gillborn, *Racism and Education*.

6. hooks, *Teaching to Transgress*, 177.

7. Mirza, *Young, Female and Black*.

8. Pennant, *Babygirl, You've Got This!*

9. Taneja-Johansson, "Whose voices are being heard?"

10. Gibbs, "Australian Adolescent Boys with Attention Deficit/Hyperactivity Disorder."

11. Zimmermann, "Looking for Trouble."

12. Hall, "Race, Articulation and Societies Structured in Dominance," 205.

13. Gelder, "Wales to Make Teaching Black, Asian and Minority Ethnic Histories Mandatory in Schools."

14. Lewis and Pearce, "High Attaining Students, Marketisation and the Absence of Care."

15. Hannah, "Harmful and Unnecessary: The Case for Abolishing Exams."

16. Coard, *How the West Indian Child Is Made Educationally Subnormal in the British School System*.

Chapter 5: A Design for Life

1. Fúnez-Flores, "Decolonial and Ontological Challenges in Social and Anthropological Theory"; see also Bhambra, "Postcolonial and Decolonial Dialogues."

2. Bhandar and Ziadah, eds., *Revolutionary Feminisms*.

3. Fanon, *Black Skin, White Masks*.

4. Hutcheon and Lashewicz, "Tracing and Troubling Continuities between Ableism and Colonialism in Canada."

5. Sharpe, *In the Wake*.

6. The feudal structuration of society was determined by the holding and leasing of land, military service in return for land tax justice, and tenants-in-chief. The king had ultimate power.

7. Virdee, "Racialized Capitalism."

8. Go, "Thinking Against Empire."

9. Shilliam and Renwick, *Squalor*.

10. Oates, *The Fires of Jubilee*.

11. James, *The Black Jacobins*.

12. *The Life and History of Swing*.

13. Trafford, *The Empire at Home*.

14. Cleall, "Disability and Otherness in the British Empire."

15. Tyler, *Social Abjection and Resistance in Neoliberal Britain*.

16. Hall et al., *Policing the Crisis.*

17. Lewis and Arday, "We'll See Things They'll Never See."

18. Younis, *The Muslim, State and Mind: Psychology in Times of Islamophobia.*

19. Fuchs, *Communication and Capitalism.*

20. Adam-Bagley, "Neurodiversity as Status Group, and as a Class-within-a-Class."

21. Tink, "'If You're Different, Are You the Same?'"

22. Healing Justice London, "Deaths by Welfare Project."

23. Mills, "How the DWP fought to Withhold Evidence Its Policies Kill Disabled People."

24. Hall, "People with Dyslexia Have Skills that We Need, Says GCHQ."

25. Bank of America, "The Value of Hiring People Who Think differently."

26. Wise, "Neurodivergent People 'Being Financially Harmed by Banks.'"

27. Jolly, "Barclays, HSBC and Lloyds among UK Banks that Had Links to Slavery."

28. White, "Terraformed: Young Black Lives in the Inner City."

29. See for example, Davidson, "Cripping Consensus," Hickman and Serlin, "Towards a Crip Methodology," Lewis, "Crip," and McRuer, "Crip."

Chapter 6: Everything Is Everything

1. *The Miseducation of Lauryn Hill* (1988) Ruffhouse Records.

2. Chapman and Carel, "Neurodiversity, Epistemic Injustice, and the Good Human Life."

3. Skeggs, "Values Beyond Value? Is Anything Beyond the Logic of Capital?" 13.

4. Hirsch, "The UK's Inadequate and Unfair Safety Net."

5. Fuller, Christian. "Parents Call for Apology over SEND Comments."

6. An Education, Health and Care Plan (EHCP) is a legal document that outlines the needs of a child or young person with special educational needs and disabilities (SEN).

7. Nevett, "Parents Urge Councillors to Apologise Over Special Needs Comments."

8. Shilliam, *Race and the Undeserving Poor.*

9. Shilliam, *Race and the Undeserving Poor.*

10. Dadzie, *Blood Sweat and Tears.*

11. Young, *The Rise of the Meritocracy.*

12. Allen, "Michael Young's The Rise of the Meritocracy."

13. Khan, "The Sociology of Elites."

Chapter 7: For Tomorrow

1. Schalk, *Black Disability Politics.*
2. World Health Organization, "Ageing."
3. Centre for Ageing Better, "The State of Ageing 2022."
4. Karpusheff, "Who Is More Likely to Lose in the Postcode Lottery of Health?"
5. Karpusheff, "Who Is More Likely to Lose in the Postcode Lottery of Health?"
6. Roberts and Taylor, "New Evidence on Disability Benefit Claims in Britain."
7. Hudson, "Thatcherism and Its Geographical Legacies"; also Uddin, Md. Kamal, "Covid-19 Response: The Global North South Divide."
8. https://www.georgepadmoreinstitute.org/collections/black-parents -movement-1969-1993.

Afterword

1. Chapman, *Empire of Normality.*
2. "Subnormal: A British Scandal." Directed / produced by Lyttanya Shannon, BBC TV Documentary, May 2021. https://www.bbc.co.uk/programmes/m000w81h
3. John-Baptiste, "The Black Children Wrongly Sent to 'Special' Schools in the 1970s."
4. Tomlinson, S. *Educational Subnormality.*
5. "Sideways" podcast. Episode 65, "Divergent Histories." Presented by Matthew Syed. Directed by Tej Adeleye and Tom Wright. BBC Radio 4, August 21, 2024. https://www.bbc.co.uk/programmes/m00224jq.
6. "Subnormal: A British Scandal." Directed / produced by Lyttanya Shannon, BBC TV Documentary, May 2021. https://www.bbc.co.uk/programmes/m000w81hl.
7. Weale, "Black People Who Were Labelled Awkward as Children Seek Justice for Lifelong Trauma."
8. *The Voice* is a British national African-Caribbean newspaper founded in 1982.

BIBLIOGRAPHY

Adam-Bagley, C. "Neurodiversity as Status Group, and as a Class-within-a-Class: Critical Realism and Dyslexia," *Open Journal of Social Sciences* 10 (2022): 117–129.

Alexander, Jeffrey C. *Action and Its Environments: Toward a New Synthesis*. New York: Columbia University Press, 1988.

Allen, Angsar. "Michael Young's *The Rise of the Meritocracy*: A Philosophical Critique," *British Journal of Educational Studies* 59 no. 4 (2011): 367–382. http://www.jstor.org/stable/41427674.

Alston, Philip. "Statement on Visit to the United Kingdom," November 2018, https://www.ohchr.org/sites/default/files/Documents/Issues/Poverty/EOM_GB_16Nov2018.pdf.

Archer, Margaret. *Structure, Agency and the Internal Conversation*. Cambridge University Press, 2014.

Aubrecht, Katie. "Disability Studies and the Language of Mental Illness," *Review of Disability Studies* 8, no. 2 (2014).

Back, Les. "Why Everyday Life Matters: Class, Community and Making Life Liveable," *Sociology* 49, no. 5 (2015): 820–836.

Bailey, Di, Wright, Nicola, and Kemp, Linda. "Self-Harm in Young People: A Challenge for General Practice," *British Journal of General Practice* 67, 665 (2017): 542–543. https://doi:10.3399/bjgp17X693545.

Bailkin, Jordanna. *The Afterlife of Empire*. Berkeley: University of California Press, 2012.

Bank of America. "The Value of Hiring People Who Think differently." Accessed May 17, 2024. https://about.bankofamerica.com/en/making-an-impact/neurodiversity-in-the-workplace.

Berger, Peter, and Luckmann, Thomas. *The Social Construction of Reality*. Garden City, NJ: Doubleday, 1966.

Bertilsdotter Rosqvist, Hanna, Hultman, Lill, Österborg Wiklund, Sofia, Nygren, Anna, Storm, Palle, and Sandberg, Greta. "Naming Ourselves, Becoming Neurodivergent

Scholars," *Disability and Society* (October 2023): 1–20. https://doi.org/10.1080/09687599.2023.2271155.

Bhambra, Gurminder K. "Postcolonial and Decolonial Dialogues," *Postcolonial Studies* 17, no. 2 (2014): 115–121.

Bhandar, Brenna, and Rafeef Ziadah, eds. *Revolutionary Feminisms: Conversations on Collective Action and Radical Thought.* London: Verso, 2020.

Booth, Robert. "UK 'in Violation of International Law' Over Poverty Levels, says UN Envoy," *The Guardian*, November 5, 2023. https://www.theguardian.com/society/2023/nov/05/uk-poverty-levels-simply-not-acceptable-says-un-envoy-olivier-de-schutter.

Brissett-Bailey, Marcia. *Black, Brilliant and Dyslexic.* UK: Jessica Kingsley Publishing, 2023.

Brown, Brené. "Brené with Lisa Lahey on Immunity to Change, Part 1 of 2," Podcast, 2024. https://brenebrown.com/podcast/immunity-to-change-part-1-of-2/.

Brown, Lydia X. Z., Ashkenazy, E., and Morenike, Giwa Onaiwu, eds. *All the Weight of Our Dreams.* Dragon Bee Press, 2017.

Bryan, Beverley, Dadzie, Stella, and Scafe, Suzanne. *The Heart of the Race: Black Women's Lives in Britain.* London: Virago, [1985] 2018.

Burawoy, Michael. "For Public Sociology," *American Sociological Review* 70, no. 1 (February 2005): 4–28. https://doi.org/10.1177/000312240507000102.

Butler, Judith. *Frames of War: When Is Life Grievable?* New York: Verso, 2009.

Cage, Eilidh, and Troxell-Whitman, Zoe. "Understanding the Reasons, Contexts and Costs of Camouflaging for Autistic Adults," *Journal of Autism and Developmental Disorders* 49, no. 5, 2019: 1899–1911.

Campanella, Mario. "Syd Barrett: Was He Suffering from Schizophrenia or Asperger's Syndrome?" *Clinical Neuropsychiatry* 12 (2015): 73–76.

Centre for Ageing Better. "The State of Ageing 2022," March 2022. https//ageing-better.org.uk.

Chapman, Robert. "Neurodiversity Theory and Its Discontents: Autism, Schizophrenia, and the Social Model." In *The Bloomsbury Companion to the Philosophy of Psychiatry,* edited by Serife Tekin and Robyn Bluhm, chapter 18. London: Bloomsbury, 2019.

———*Empire of Normality: Neurodiversity and Capitalism.* London: Pluto Press, 2023.

Chapman, Robert, and Carel, Havi. "Neurodiversity, Epistemic Injustice, and the Good Human Life," *Journal of Social Philosophy* 53, no. 4 (2022): 614–631. https://doi.org/10.1111/josp.12456.

Cleall, Esme. "Disability and Otherness in the British Empire: Disablement as a Discourse of Difference." In Cleall, Esme, *Colonising Disability: Impairment and*

Otherness Across Britain and Its Empire, c. 1800–1914. Critical Perspectives on Empire, pp. 25–61. Cambridge University Press, 2022.

———*Colonising Disability: Impairment and Otherness Across Britain and Its Empire, c. 1800–1914. Critical Perspectives on Empire.* Cambridge University Press, 2022.

Clemons, Kristal Moore. "Black Feminist Thought and Qualitative Research in Education," *Oxford Research Encyclopedia of Education* August 28, 2019. https://doi.org/10.1093/acrefore/9780190264093.013.1194.

Coard, Bernard. *How the West Indian Child Is Made Educationally Subnormal in the British School System.* Birmingham: Mc Dermott Publishing, 1971.

Coker, Tumaini R., Elliott, Marc N., Toomey, Sara L., Schwebel, David C., Cuccaro, Paula Tortolero, Susan E., Davies, Susan L., Visser, Susanna N., Schuster, Mark A. "Racial and Ethnic Disparities in ADHD Diagnosis and Treatment," *Pediatrics* 138, no. 3 (2016). doi: 10.1542/peds.2016-0407.

Cooper, Brittany. *Eloquent Rage: A Black Feminist Discovers Her Superpower.* New York: St Martin's Press, 2018.

Dadzie, Stella. *Blood Sweat and Tears. A Report of the Bede Anti-Racist Detached Youth Work Project.* Leicester: Youth Work Press, 1997.

Davidson, Michael. "Cripping Consensus: Disability Studies at the Intersection," *American Literary History* 28, no. 2 (2016): 433–453.

Diemer, Marie Claire, Gerstein, Emily D., and April Regester. "Autism Presentation in Female and Black Populations: Examining the Roles of Identity, Theory, and Systemic Inequalities," *Autism* 26, no. 8 (July 2022). https://doi.org/10.1177/13623613221113501.

Dodd, Vikram. "Black People Nine Times More Likely to Face Stop and Search than White People," *The Guardian,* October 27 2020. https://www.theguardian.com/uk-news/2020/oct/27/black-people-nine-times-more-likely-to-face-stop-and-search-than-white-people.

Dorling, Danny. *Do We Need Economic Inequality?* Cambridge: Polity Press, 2018.

Dunkley, Elaine, McGough, Kate, and Agerholm, Harriet. "Overcrowded Specialist Schools: 'We're Teaching in Cupboards.'" BBC.co.uk, February 20, 2023. Accessed May 17, 2024. https://www.bbc.co.uk/news/education-64418797.

Durkheim, Émile. *The Division of Labor in Society.* Translated by G. Simpson. New York: The Free Press, [1893] 1965.

———*Suicide: A Study in Sociology.* Translated by J. A. Spaulding. New York: The Free Press, [1897] 1979.

Dyi Huijg, Dieuwertje. "Neuronormativity in Theorising Agency: An Argument for a Critical Neurodiversity Approach." In *Neurodiversity Studies: A New Critical Paradigm,* edited by Hanna Rosqvist, Nick Chown, and Anna Stenning. London: Routledge, 2020.

Elder-Vass, Dave. *The Causal Power of Social Structures: Emergence, Structure and Agency.* Cambridge University Press, 2010.

Eley, Adam, and Holt, Alison. "Families of Disabled People Tell BBC of Battle for NHS Care support," BBC.co.uk, February 14, 2024. Accessed May 17, 2024. https://www.bbc.co.uk/news/health-68238040.

Ellis, Katie, Garland-Thompson, Rosemary, Kent, Mike, and Robertson, Rachel, eds. *Looking Towards the Future. Vol. 2 of Interdisciplinary Approaches to Disability Studies.* New York: Routledge, 2018.

The Equality Trust. "The Scale of Economic Inequality in the UK." https://equalitytrust.org.uk/scale-economic-inequality-uk. Accessed May 18 2024.

Fanon, Frantz. *The Wretched of the Earth.* Translated by Constance Farrington. London: Penguin, 2001.

———*Black Skin, White Masks.* London: Penguin, 2021.

Freire, Paulo. *Pedagogy of the Oppressed.* London: Penguin Books Ltd, 1996.

Fuchs, Christian. *Communication and Capitalism: A Critical Theory.* University of Westminster Press, 2020. https://doi.org/10.2307/j.ctv12fw7t5.

Fuller, Christian. "Parents Call for Apology over SEND Comments." *BBC.co.uk,* May 16 2023. Accessed May 17, 2024. https://www.bbc.co.uk/news/articles/c721lev4x84o.

Fúnez-Flores, Jairo I. "Decolonial and Ontological Challenges in Social and Anthropological Theory," *Theory, Culture and Society* 39, no.6 (2022): 21–41.

Gelder, Sam. "Wales to Make Teaching Black, Asian and Minority Ethnic Histories Mandatory in Schools," *Big Issue,* October 1, 2021. https://www.bigissue.com /news/wales-to-make-teaching-black-asian-and-minority-ethnic-histories -mandatory-in-schools/.

Gibbs, Kathryn. "Australian Adolescent Boys with Attention Deficit/Hyperactivity Disorder (AD/HD): Teacher and Teaching Factors that Assess the Efficacy of Reducing Unwanted Behaviours within the Classroom Environment," *Australian Journal of Learning Difficulties* 23, no. 1 (2018): 53–65. https://doi.org/10.1080 /19404158.2017.1393626.

Giddens, Anthony. *Central Problems in Social Theory: Action, Structure and Contradiction in Social Analysis.* Berkeley: University of California Press, 1979.

Gillborn, David. *Racism and Education: Coincidence or Conspiracy?* London: Routledge, 2008.

Go, Julian. "Thinking Against Empire: Anticolonial Thought as Social Theory," *British Journal of Sociology* 74, no. 3 (2023): 275–526. https://doi.org/10.1111/1468 -4446.12993.

Goodley Dan. "Towards Socially Just Pedagogies: Deleuzoguattarian Critical Disability Studies," *International Journal of Inclusive Education* 11, no. 3 (2007): 317–334.

———"Dis/entangling Critical Disability Studies," *Disability and Society* 28, no. 5 (September 2012): 631–644. https://doi:10.1080/09687599.2012.717884.

Goodley, Dan, Liddiard, Kirsty, and Runswick-Cole, Katherine. "Feeling Disability: Theories of Affect and Critical Disability Studies," *Disability and Society* 33, no. 2 (November 2017). https://doi.10.1080/09687599.2017.1402752.

Gorton, Kristyn. "Theorizing Emotion and Affect: Feminist Engagements," *Feminist Theory* 8, no. 3 (2007). https://doi.org/10.1177/1464700107082369.

Gramsci, Antonio. *Selections from the Prison Notebooks of Antonio Gramsci.* New York, International Publishers, 1971.

Grant, Tyla. "Neurodivergent Black Girls Don't Get the Same Help: My Journey to Becoming an Autism Advocate," blackballad.co.uk, December 17 2020. https://blackballad.co.uk/views-voices/neurodivergent-black-girls-autism?listIds =598b26616409a286334e51bc.

Hall, Rachel. "People with Dyslexia Have Skills that We Need, Says GCHQ." *The Guardian*, April 29, 2021. https://www.theguardian.com/uk-news/2021/apr/29 /people-with-dyslexia-have-skills-that-we-need-says-gchq.

Hall, Stuart. "Race, the Floating Signifier." Media Education Foundation Transcript, 1997. https://www.mediaed.org/transcripts/Stuart-Hall-Race-the-Floating -Signifier-Transcript.pdf.

———"Race, Articulation and Societies Structured in Dominance (1980)," in *Essential Essays Volume 1.* Duke University Press, 2019.

———*Essential Essays Volume 1*, edited by David Morley. Duke University Press, 2019.

———"Whites of Their Eyes: Racist Ideologies and the Media." In *Selected writings on Race and Difference*, edited by Paul Gilmore and Ruth Wilson Gilmore. Duke University Press, [1981] 2021. https://doi.org/10.1215/9781478021223-009.

Hall, Stuart, Critcher, Chas, Jefferson, Tony, Clarke, John N., and Roberts, Brian. *Policing the Crisis: Mugging, the State, and Law and Order.* London: Macmillan, 1978.

Hannah, John. "Harmful and Unnecessary: The Case for Abolishing Exams," *About Campus* 24, no. 2 (2019): 12–17. https://doi.org/10.1177/1086482219870000.

Healing Justice London. "Deaths by Welfare Project." 2022. https://healingjusticeldn .org/deaths-by-welfare-project/.

Hedley, Darren, Cassidy, Sarah, Templin, Chris, Hayward, Susan M., Haschek, Alex, Bulluss, Erin, Den Houting, Jac, Kõlves, Kairi, Maddox, Brenna B., Morgan, Lisa, et al. "Recommendations from the 2021 Australasian Society for Autism Research." Paper presented at Health, Wellbeing and Suicide Prevention in Autism Conference and Roundtable. La Trobe University, Melbourne, 2000. https://doi 10.26181/19690432.

Hickman, Louise, and Serlin, David. "Towards a Crip Methodology for Critical Disability Studies." In *Looking Towards the Future*. Vol. 2 *of Interdisciplinary Approaches to Disability Studies*, edited by Katie Ellis, Rosemary Garland-Thompson, Mike Kent and Rachel Robertson, pp. 131–141. New York: Routledge, 2018.

Hill Collins, Patricia. "Black Feminist Thought in the Matrix of Domination." In *Black Feminist Thought: Knowledge, Consciousness, and the Politics of Empowerment* pp. 221–238, London: Harper Collins, 1990. https://archive.cunyhumanitiesalliance .org/introsocspring20/wp-content/uploads/sites/50/2019/03/Collins.Black -Feminist-Thought.pdf.

———*Black Feminist Thought, 30th Anniversary Edition: Knowledge, Consciousness and the Politics of Empowerment*. Milton: Taylor and Francis, 2021.

———*Black Feminist Thought: Knowledge, Consciousness, and the Politics of Empowerment*. New York: Routledge, 2000.

Hinshaw, Stephen P., Owens, Elizabeth B., Zalecki, Christine, Huggins, Suzanne Perrigue, Montenegro-Nevado, Adriana J., Schrodek, Emily, and Swanson, Erika N. "Prospective Follow-up of Girls with Attention-Deficit/Hyperactivity Disorder into Early Adulthood: Continuing Impairment Includes Elevated Risk for Suicide Attempts and Self-injury," *Journal of Consulting and Clinical Psychology* 80, no. 6 (2012): 1041–1051.

Hirsch, Donald. "The UK's Inadequate and Unfair Safety Net." abrdn Financial Fairness Trust Briefing Paper, January 2024. https://www.financialfairness.org.uk /docs?editionId=c9f66338-7c19-4ee8-8634-b0f800c19dc6.

hooks, bell. *All about Love: New Visions*. US: William Morrow and Co., 2000.

———*Feminism Is for Everybody: Passionate Politics*. London: Pluto Press, 2000.

———*Outlaw Culture*. New York: Routledge, 1994.

———*Teaching to Transgress: Education as the Practice of Freedom*. London: Routledge, 1994.

Hudson, Ray. "Thatcherism and Its Geographical Legacies: The New Map of Socio-Spatial Inequality in the Divided Kingdom," *The Geographical Journal* 179, no. 4 (2013): 377–381.

Hutcheon, Emily J., and Lashewicz, Bonnie. "Tracing and Troubling Continuities between Ableism and Colonialism in Canada," *Disability and Society* 35, no. 5 (2020): 695–714. https://doi: 10.1080/09687599.2019.1647145.

Institute of Race Relations. "BME Statistics on Poverty and Deprivation." Accessed January 29, 2024. https://irr.org.uk/research/statistics/poverty/#:~:text =Furthermore%2C%20people%20in%20Black%20and,than%20people%20 in%20White%20families.

James, C.L.R. *The Black Jacobins: Toussaint L'Ouverture and the San Domingo Revolution*. Penguin Modern Classics, 2022.

John-Baptiste, Ashley. "The Black Children Wrongly Sent to 'Special' Schools in the 1970s." *BBC.co.uk*, May 20, 2021. https://www.bbc.co.uk/news/uk-57099654.

Johnson, Merri L. "Neuroqueer Feminism: Turning with Tenderness to Borderline Personality Disorder," *Journal of Women in Culture and Society* 46 no. 3 (spring 2021): 635–662.

Jolly, Jasper. "Barclays, HSBC and Lloyds among UK Banks that Had Links to Slavery," *The Guardian*, June 18, 2020. https://www.theguardian.com/business/2020/jun/18/barclays-hsbc-and-lloyds-among-uk-banks-that-had-links-to-slavery.

Karpusheff, Justine. "Who Is More Likely to Lose in the Postcode Lottery of Health?" Accessed May 10, 2024. https://www.health.org.uk/news-and-comment/blogs/who-is-more-likely-to-lose-in-the-postcode-lottery-of-health.

Khan, S. Rahman. "The Sociology of Elites," *Annual Review of Sociology* 38 (2012): 361–377.

Kõlves, Kairi, Fitzgerald, Cecilie, Nordentoft, Merete, Wood, Stephen J., and Erlangsen, Annette. "Assessment of Suicidal Behaviors Among Individuals with Autism Spectrum Disorder in Denmark," *JAMA Netw Open* 4, no. 1 (January 2021).

Kumari Campbell, Fiona A. "Inciting Legal Fictions: Disability's Date with Ontology and the Ableist Body of the Law," *Griffith Law Review* 10 (2001): 42–62.

———— "Exploring Internalized Ableism Using Critical Race Theory," *Disability and Society* 23, no. 2 (March 2008). https://doi:10.1080/09687590701841190.

Lam, Lawrence T. "Attention Deficit Disorder and Hospitalization Owing to Intra- and Interpersonal Violence among Children and Young Adolescents," *Journal of Adolescent Health* 36, no. 1 (January 2005): 19–24.

Lange, Matthew. *Lineages of Despotism and Development: British Colonialism and State Power*. Chicago: University of Chicago Press, 2009.

Langenhoven, Ruben, Fouché, Paul, and Naidoo, Pravani. "The Psychosocial Personality Development of Syd Barrett." Dissertation, University of the Free State, Bloemfontein, 2019. 10.13140/RG.2.2.10783.43686.

Lentin, Alana. *Why Race Still Matters*. Cambridge, UK: Polity Press.

Lewis, V. A. "Crip." In *Keywords for Disability Studies*, edited by Rachel Adams, Benjamin Weiss, and David Serlin. pp. 46–48. New York University Press, 2015.

Lewis, Chantelle Jessica, and Arday, Jason. "We'll See Things They'll Never See: Sociological Reflections on Race, Neurodiversity and Higher Education," *The Sociological Review* 71, no. 6 (July 2023). https://doi.org/10.1177/00380261231184357.

Lewis, Chantelle Jessica, and Kerkhoff-Parnell, Bryel. 2024. "Conceptualising Black (Co-) Reflexive Feminist Methodologies: Collaboration, Process and Critical Friendship." *Sociology* 0(0). https://doi.org/10.1177/00380385241295664.

Lewis, Kirstin, and Pearce, Sarah. "High Attaining Students, Marketisation and the Absence of Care: Everyday Experiences in an Urban Academy," *Pedagogy, Culture and Society* 30, no. 2 (2022): 261–280. https://doi.org/10.1080/14681366.2020.1801811.

The Life and History of Swing. The Kent Rick-Burner. Written by Himself. London: R.Carlile, 1830.

Loja, Ema, Costa, Maria Emília, Hughes, Bill, and Menezes, Isabel. "Disability, Embodiment and Ableism: Stories of Resistance," *Disability and Society* 28, no. 2 (August 2012): 190–203. https://doi: 10.1080/09687599.2012.705057.

Lundberg, D. J., and Chen, J. A. "Structural Ableism in Public Health and Healthcare: a Definition and Conceptual Framework," *The Lancet Regional Health - Americas* 30 February 2024.

Marczak, Nikki, and Shields, Kirril. *Genocide Perspectives VI: The Process and the Personal Cost of Genocide.* Sydney: UTS ePRESS, 2020. https://doi.org/10.5130/aaf.

Marx, Karl. *The Eighteenth Brumaire of Louis Bonaparte.* New York: Marx–Engels Internet Archive [1852] 2010. https://www.marxists.org/archive/marx/works/download/pdf/18th-Brumaire.pdf.

Maté, Gabe. *Scattered Minds: A New Look at the Origins and Healing of Attention Deficit Disorder.* Toronto: A.A. Knopf, 1999.

———*In the Realm of Hungry Ghosts: Close Encounters with Addiction.* Toronto: A.A. Knopf, 2008.

Maté, Gabe, and Maté, Daniel. *The Myth of Normal: Trauma, Illness and Healing in a Toxic Culture.* Toronto: A.A. Knopf, 2022.

McRuer, Robert. "Crip," in *Keywords for Radicals: The Contested Vocabulary of Late Capitalist Struggle,* edited by Kelly Frisch, Clare O'Connor, and A. K. Thompson, pp. 18–24. Chicago University Press, 2016.

Meer, Nasar, and Holmwood, John. "John Holmwood: Sociology of Structure, Sociology as Structure," *Sociology* 50, no. 5 (October 2016). https://www.jstor.org/stable/26556382.

Metzl, Jonathan. *The Protest Psychosis: How Schizophrenia Became a Black Disease.* Boston: Beacon, 2009.

Mills, Charles Wright. *The Sociological Imagination.* Oxford University Press, [1959] 2000.

Mills, China. "How the DWP Fought to Withhold Evidence Its Policies Kill Disabled People." November 22, 2023. https://www.opendemocracy.net/en/dwp-disability-benefits-jeremy-hunt-autumn-statement/.

Mirza, Heidi Safia. *Young, Female and Black.* Abingdon: Routledge, 1992.

Mohdin, Aamna, and Gentleman, Amelia. "UK Failing to Address Systemic Racism against Black People, says UN Expert." *The Guardian,* January 27, 2023. https://www.theguardian.com/world/2023/jan/27/uk-government-failing-to-address

-systemic-racism-against-black-people-un-working-group-of-experts-on-people
-of-african-descent.

Mollow, Anna. "'When Black Women Start Going on Prozac': Race, Gender, and
Mental Illness in and Meri Nana-Ama Danquah's Willow Weep for Me," *MELUS31*
3 (2006): 67–99.

Morrison, Toni. *The Bluest Eye*. Vintage Books, 1999.

Mundasad, Smitha. "Black Women Four Times More Likely to Die in Childbirth."
BBC.co.uk, 11 November 2021. https://www.bbc.co.uk/news/health-59248345.

Naghavi, M., on behalf of the Global Burden of Disease Self-Harm Collaborators.
"Global, Regional, and National Burden of Suicide Mortality 1990 to 2016: Sys-
tematic Analysis for the Global Burden of Disease Study 2016," *British Medical
Journal* (February 2019); 364: l94. https://doi.org/10.1136/bmj.l94.

Nevett, Joshua. "Parents Urge Councillors to Apologise over Special Needs Comments," BBC.co.uk, February 6, 2024. Accessed 17 May 2024. https://www.bbc
.co.uk/news/uk-england-coventry-warwickshire-68212512.

Ngcobo, Lauretta, ed. *Let It Be Told: Black Women Writers in Britain*. London: Virago,
1988.

Noor, Syafiq Mat, and Azyan Shafee, "The Role of Critical Friends in Action Research: A Framework for Design and Implementation," *Practitioner Research* 3
(July 2021): 1–33. https://doi.org/10.32890/pr2021.3.

Oates, Stephen B. *The Fires of Jubilee: Nat Turner's Fierce Rebellion*. Perrenial, 2004.

Patterson, Nia. "Nia's Autism Story," Healthline.com, February 20, 2023. https://www
.healthline.com/health/adhd/nias-adhd-autism-story.

Pennant, April-Louise M. *Babygirl, You've Got This! Experiences of Black Girls and
Women in the English Education System*. London: Bloomsbury Academic, 2024.
https://www.bloomsbury.com/uk/babygirl-youve-got-this-9781350279001/.

Pickens, Théri A. *Black Madness:: Mad Blackness*. Durham N.C.: Duke University
Press, 2019.

Pollak, Yehuda, Shoham, Rachel, Dayan, Haym, Gabrieli-Seri, Ortal, and Berger, Itai.
"Symptoms of ADHD Predict Lower Adaptation to the COVID-19 Outbreak:
Financial Decline, Low Adherence to Preventive Measures, Psychological
Distress, and Illness-Related Negative Perceptions," *Journal of Attention Disorders*
26, no. 5 (2022): 735–746.

Poppel, Frans van, and Day, Lincoln H. "A Test of Durkheim's Theory of Suicide—
Without Committing the 'Ecological Fallacy,'" *American Sociological Review* 61,
no. 3 (1996): 500–507. https://doi.org/10.2307/2096361.

Radulski, Elizabeth. "Conceptualising Autistic Masking, Camouflaging, and Neurotypical Privilege: Towards a Minority Group Model of Neurodiversity," *Human
Development* 66, no. 2 (2022): 113–127. https://doi.org/10.1159/000524122.

Reynolds, Tracey. "Re-thinking a Black Feminist Standpoint," *Ethnic and Racial Studies* 25, no. 4 (April 2020). https://doi.org/10.1080/01419870220136709.

Roberts, Jennifer, and Taylor, Karl. "New Evidence on Disability Benefit Claims in Britain: The Role of Health and the Local Labour Market," *Economica* 89, 353 (2021): 131–160.

Robinson, Cedric. J. *Black Marxism: The Making of the Black Radical Tradition*. Revised and updated 3rd Edition. University of North Carolina Press, 2021.

Rohn, R. D., Sarles, R. M., Kenn, T. J., Reynolds, B. J., Heald, F. P. "Adolescents Who Attempt Suicide," *Journal of Pediatrics* 90, no. 4 (1977): 636–638.

Rosqvist, Hanna, Chown, Nick, and Stenning, Anna, eds. *Neurodiversity Studies: A New Critical Paradigm*. London: Routledge, 2020.

Runswick-Cole, Katherine. "'Us' and 'Them': The Limits and Possibilities of a Politics of Neurodiversity in Neoliberal Times," *Disability and Society* 29, no. 7 (2014): 1117–1129. https://doi:10.1080/09687599.2014.910107.

Schalk, Sami. *Black Disability Politics*. Duke University Press, 2022.

Schwartz-Johnston, Ramona M. "Ableism, Personhood, and Communication for People Who Don't Speak," *Peace Review* 31, no. 4 (2019): 479–486. Doi: 10.1080 /10402659.2019.1800934.

Selvin, H. "Durkheim's Suicide: Further Thoughts on a Methodological Classic." In Robert Nisbet, ed. *Émile Durkheim*. Englewood Cliffs, NJ: Prentice-Hall, 1965.

Sharpe, Christina. *In the Wake: On Blackness and Being*. Duke University Press, 2016.

Shaw, Philip, Stringaris, Argyris, Nigg, Joel, and Leibenluft, Ellen. "Emotion Dysregulation in Attention Deficit Hyperactivity Disorder," *The American Journal of Psychiatry* 171, no. 3 (2014): 276–293.

Shilliam, Robbie. *Race and the Undeserving Poor: From Abolition to Brexit*. Columbia University Press, 2018.

Shilliam, Robbie, and Renwick, Daniel. *Squalor*. Columba University Press, 2022.

Sinclair, Jim. "Don't Mourn for Us," *Our Voice* 1 no. 3 (1993) https://www.autreat .com/dont_mourn.html.

Skeggs, Bev. "Values Beyond Value? Is Anything Beyond the Logic of Capital?" *The British Journal of Sociology* 65, no. 1 (2014): 1–20. https://doi.org/10.1111/1468 -4446.12072.

Sobande, Francesca. *The Digital Lives of Black Women in Britain*. Chester UK: Palgrave Macmillan, 2020.

———*Consuming Crisis: Commodifying Care and COVID-19*. SAGE Publications Ltd., 2022.

Stenning, Anna, and Bertilsdotter Rosqvist, Hanna. "Neurodiversity Studies: Mapping Out Possibilities of a New Critical Paradigm," *Disability and Society* 36, no. 9 (June 2021): 1532–1537. https://doi:10.1080/09687599.2021.1919503.

Stewart, Mary E., Barnard, Louise, Pearson, Joanne, Hasan, Reem, and O'Brien, Gregory. "Presentation of Depression in Autism and Asperger Syndrome," *Autism* 10, no.1(January, 2006): 103–16. https://doi:10.1177/1362361306060620-3.

Swartz, Sally. "Feminism and Psychiatric Diagnosis: Reflections of a Feminist Practitioner," *Feminism and Psychology* 23, no.1 (2013): 41–48.

Taneja-Johansson, Shruti. "Whose Voices Are Being Heard? A Scoping Review of Research on School Experiences Among Persons with Autism and Attention Deficit/Hyperactivity Disorder," *Emotional and Behavioural Difficulties* 28, no. 1 (2023): 32–51. https://doi.org/10.1080/13632752.2023.2202441.

Thomas, Carol. *Female Forms: Experiencing and Understanding Disability*. Buckingham: The Open University Press, 1999.

Thompson, Edward P. *The Making of the English Working Class*. Littlehampton Book Services, 1963.

Tink, Amanda. "'If You're Different Are You the Same?': The Nazi Genocide of Disabled People and Les Murray's Fredy Neptune." In Nikki Marczak and Kirril Shields, eds. *Genocide Perspectives VI: The Process and the Personal Cost of Genocide*. Sydney: UTS ePRESS, 2020. https://doi.org/10.5130/aaf.

Titchkosky, Tanya. "Disability, a Rose by Any Other Name? People-first language in Canadian Society," *The Canadian Review of Sociology and Anthropology* 38, no. 2 (2001): 125–140.

Tomlinson, Sally. *Educational Subnormality: A Study in Decision-Making*. London: Routledge, [1981] 2012.

Trafford, James. *The Empire at Home: Internal Colonies and the End of Britain*. London: Pluto Press, 2021.

Tyler, Imogen. *Social Abjection and Resistance in Neoliberal Britain*. London: Zed Books, 2022.

———*Stigma: The Machinery of Inequality*. London: Bloomsbury, 2022.

Uddin, Md. Kamal. "Covid-19 Response: The Global North South Divide," *World Affairs: The Journal of International Issues* 25, no. 3 (Autumn 2021): 142–153.

Virdee, Satnam. "Racialized Capitalism: An Account of Its Contested Origins and Consolidation," *The Sociological Review* 67, no.1 (2019): 3–27.

Weale, Sally. "Black People Who Were Labelled Awkward as Children Seek Justice for Lifelong Trauma," *The Guardian*, Feb 21, 2023. https://www.theguardian.com /education/2023/feb/21/black-people-labelled-backward-as-children-seek -justice-for-lifelong-trauma.

White, J. "Terraformed: Young Black Lives in the Inner City." Transcript, 2024. https://www.ucl.ac.uk/racism-racialisation/transcript-terraformed-young-black-lives-inner-city.

Williams, Eric. *Capitalism and Slavery.* Penguin Modern Classics, [1944] 2022.

Wilson-Gilmore, Ruth. *Golden Gulag. Prisons, Surplus, Crisis, and Opposition in Globalizing California.* University of California Press.

Wise, Anna. "Neurodivergent People 'Being Financially Harmed by Banks,'" *The Independent,* May 29, 2023. https://www.independent.co.uk/money/neurodivergent-people-being-financially-harmed-by-banks-b2347485.html.

Wong, Alice. *Disability Visibility: First-Person Stories from the Twenty-first Century.* London: Vintage, 2020.

World Health Organization. "Ageing." Accessed May 17, 2024. https://www.who.int/health-topics/ageing#tab=tab_1.

———"Mental Health and Substance Use." Accessed May 17, 2024. https://www.who.int/westernpacific/about/how-we-work/programmes/mental-health-and-substance-abuse.

Young, Lola. "What Is Black British Feminism?" *Women: A Cultural Review* 11, no. 1–2 (January 2000): 45–60.

Young, Michael. *The Rise of the Meritocracy.* 2nd edition. London: Routledge, 1994.

Younis, Tarek. *The Muslim, State and Mind: Psychology in Times of Islamophobia.* SAGE Publications Ltd, 2023.

Zimmermann, Calvin R. "Looking for Trouble: How Teachers' Racialized Practices Perpetuate Discipline Inequities in Early Childhood," *Sociology of Education* (Feb 2024). DOI: 10.1177/00380407241228581.

INDEX

ableism, 28, 38–41; capitalism and,
132–34, 156, 171, 186, 205; damage
from, 88–90; emotional toll of, 60;
Kumari Campbell on, 6, 39; racism
and, 104, 106, 171, 186, 205, 208
accountability, 45, 57, 73–74, 84
Adeleye, Tej, 208, 210, 212
ADHD. *See* attention deficit
hyperactivity disorder
Afrocentric feminist epistemology, 45,
56, 71–74, 208
ageism, 188–90
agency, 46–54, 57–59; definitions of,
47; Dyi Huijg on, 25–26; free
market politics and, 151
Alexander, Jeffrey C., 46
Algerian independence, 34
algorithms of educational achievement, 106, 116, 123–26
Allen, Ansgar, 173
Alston, Philip, 18
Angelou, Maya, 12–13
anomie, 93–94
"anti-love," 5
Archer, Margaret, 48
artificial intelligence, 198–99
Asasumasu, Kassiane, 9–10
assimilation fatigue, 196
attention deficit disorder (ADD), 6, 10

attention deficit hyperactivity disorder
(ADHD), 10, 52, 165; autism and,
80; diagnosis of, 98; educational
system and, 110–15; emotional
dysregulation in, 84–86; suicide
risk with, 92–93
Aubrecht, Katie, 83
authenticity, 65, 85, 91, 97, 161, 181
autism, 10; ADHD and, 80; masking
of, 84–86, 95; medical models of,
161; suicide risk with, 91–95

Bagley, Adam, 143–44
Barrett, Roger Keith "Syd," 76–78
Bermudez, Trishia, 99
Bertilsdottir Rosqvist, Hanna, 52–53
Black feminism, 29–30, 36, 65–67,
168–69; Marxism and, 43–44, 56,
58, 66. *See also* gender norms
Black Lives Matter movement, 35, 166
Black Parents movement, 210, 212
Black studies, 36–38, 66
Black subjectivities, 32–36, 44, 65–67;
education and, 108–12
Blur (band), 185, 186
Brissett-Bailey, Marcia, 7
Brown, Brené, 49
Bryan, Beverley, 30
Butler, Judith, 49, 80, 90–91, 96

A NOTE ON THE TYPE

This book has been composed in Arno, an Old-style serif typeface in the
classic Venetian tradition, designed by Robert Slimbach at Adobe.

GPSR Authorized Representative: Easy Access System Europe - Mustamäe tee 50, 10621 Tallinn, Estonia, gpsr.requests@easproject.com

www.ingramcontent.com/pod-product-compliance
Ingram Content Group UK Ltd.
Pitfield, Milton Keynes, MK11 3LW, UK
UKHW041542130825
461822UK00001B/4